An Artist after All
Daniel Fowler in Canada

An Artist after All
Daniel Fowler in Canada

DOROTHY M. FARR

Agnes Etherington Art Centre, Queen's University, Kingston, Canada

For Frances

Published on the occasion of the exhibition *"An Artist After All": Daniel Fowler in Canada*,
Agnes Etherington Art Centre, Queen's University, Kingston
10 September–3 December 2006
Exhibition curated by Dorothy M. Farr

This book and the exhibition are made possible through the generous support of Frances K. Smith, the Janet Braide Memorial Fund, the Healthy Community Fund of the City of Kingston, the George Taylor Richardson Memorial Fund and the Ontario Arts Council.

ONTARIO ARTS COUNCIL
CONSEIL DES ARTS DE L'ONTARIO

Editor: Peter Smith, Brockville
Photography: Agnes Etherington Art Centre, Kingston: pages 17, 71.
Art Gallery of Ontario, Toronto: catalogue number 22.
Spencer Bardell, Kingston: catalogue numbers 10, 13, 14, 15, 21, 24, 25, 26, 29, 30, 41, 45, 51.
J. M. Brooke: page 62.
D. M. Farr: page 32.
National Gallery of Canada, Ottawa: catalogue numbers 33, 49, 52.
Queen's University Archives, Kingston: page 18.
Cheryl O'Brien: catalogue numbers 1, 34, 40, 54.
Stephen Wild, Kingston: page 20, catalogue number 31.

Design: Associés libres, Montreal
Printers: Marquis Book Printing Inc.

Library and Archives Canada Cataloguing in Publication

Farr, Dorothy "An artist after all" : Daniel Fowler in Canada / Dorothy M. Farr.

Catalogue of an exhibition held at the Agnes Etherington Art Centre, Sept. 10-Dec. 3, 2006.
Includes bibliographical references.
ISBN 1-55339-090-3

1. Fowler, Daniel, 1810-1894--Exhibitions. 2. Watercolor painting--
19th century--Canada--Exhibitions. I. Agnes Etherington Art Centre
II. Title. III. Title: Daniel Fowler in Canada.

ND1843.F58A4 2006 759.11
C2006-903428-1

Distribution: ABC ART BOOKS CANADA / ABC LIVRES D'ART CANADA
www.ABCartbookscanada.com

Agnes Etherington Art Centre, Queen's University, Kingston, Ontario, Canada, K7L 3N6
www.aeac.ca

Contents

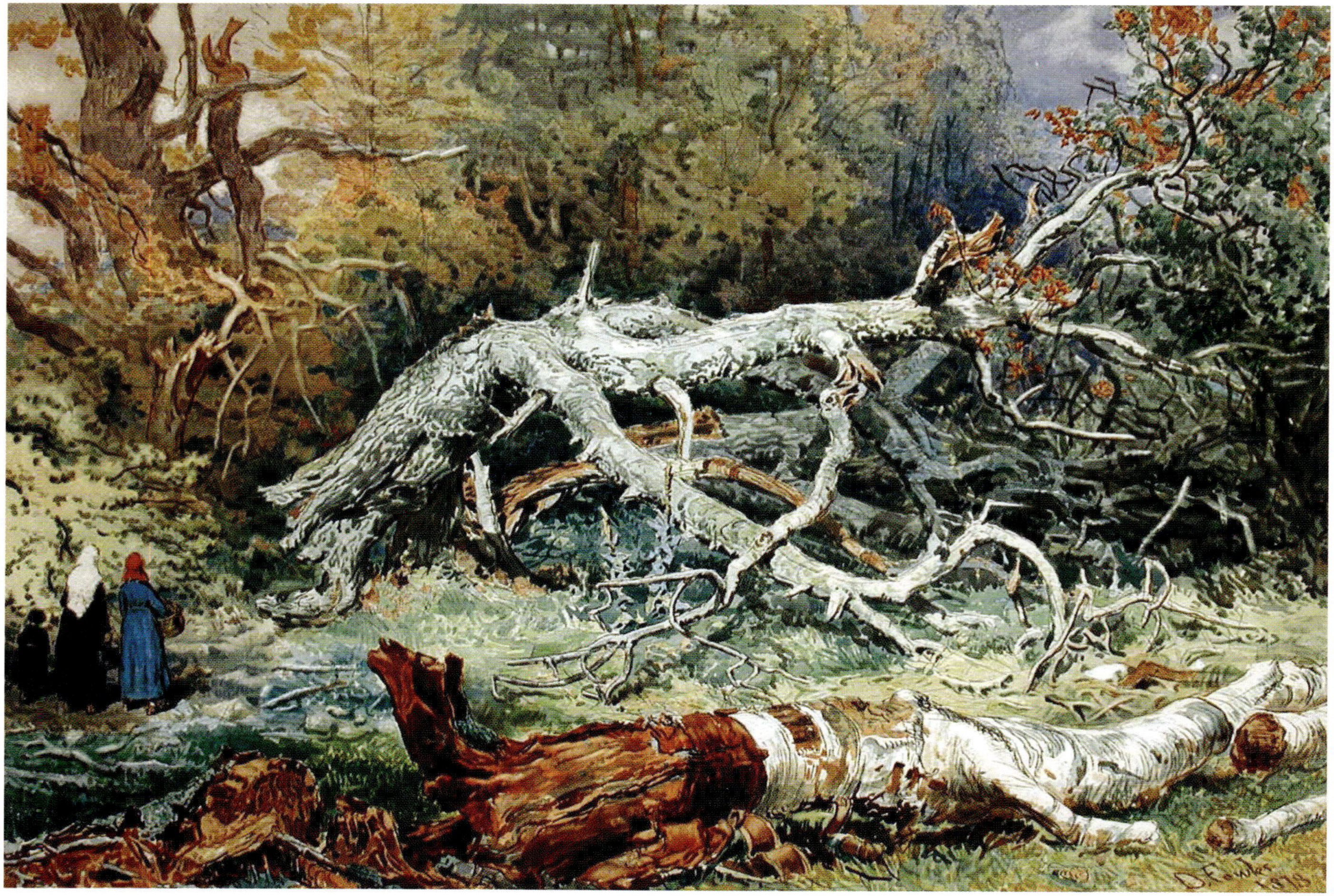

Cat. 30
Woodland Scene, 1878, Agnes Etherington Art Centre, Kingston (AEAC)

Foreword

The art of watercolour painting is much undervalued in current art history. As a paper-based medium, watercolours are normally hidden from view in the protective environment of the museum vault. Unlike drawings, watercolours are finished works of art and thus are not brought out for exhibition with related paintings. And because watercolour painting was practised by amateurs and professionals alike, art history has tended to place the medium in the margins.

Yet in the nineteenth century watercolour painting enjoyed full stature in Britain, both in the academies and in the drawing room. We need only recall the extraordinary accomplishments of J.M.W. Turner or Richard Parkes Bonington and, under their influence, Eugène Delacroix and Théodore Géricault, to know that watercolour was appreciated for its immediacy and unique expressive potential.

British-born and British-trained, Daniel Fowler emerged from that tradition and, unlike the mostly military-trained topographical watercolourists who came to Canada in the first half of the nineteenth century, seems to have brought with him the confidence that he could succeed as an artist in that medium. And although Fowler, as Art Centre curator Dorothy Farr elegantly elucidates in this catalogue, would spend many years as a farmer before returning to his brushes, he was right.

In 1979 Frances K. Smith, then curator at the Agnes Etherington Art Centre, produced the exhibition and carefully documented catalogue *Daniel Fowler of Amherst Island 1810–1894*. Today, a generation later, Dorothy Farr revisits the subject, this time exploring the relationships between Fowler's life on the land, his fascinating autobiographical and fictional writings, and his work as an artist. I thank her for the sensitivity and dedication that she has brought to her subject, which breathe throughout this publication.

While the majority of works in this exhibition and catalogue are drawn from the Art Centre's extensive Fowler holdings, I am grateful to the following institutions and individuals whose generous loans have helped us present so stellar a selection of Fowler's Canadian watercolours:

Art Gallery of Hamilton
Art Gallery of Ontario
Art Gallery of Windsor
Anna Hitchens
Mrs. John Kime
Library and Archives Canada
Carol Macfarlane
National Gallery of Canada
Roberta Reil
W. D. Jordan Special Collections and Music Library, Queen's University Libraries

Finally, to Frances K. Smith I offer my sincerest thanks not only for her landmark research some thirty years ago, and for her creation of the exhaustive Daniel Fowler Archive at the Art Centre on which subsequent Fowler students depend, but also for her generous support of this exhibition and publication.

Janet M. Brooke
Director

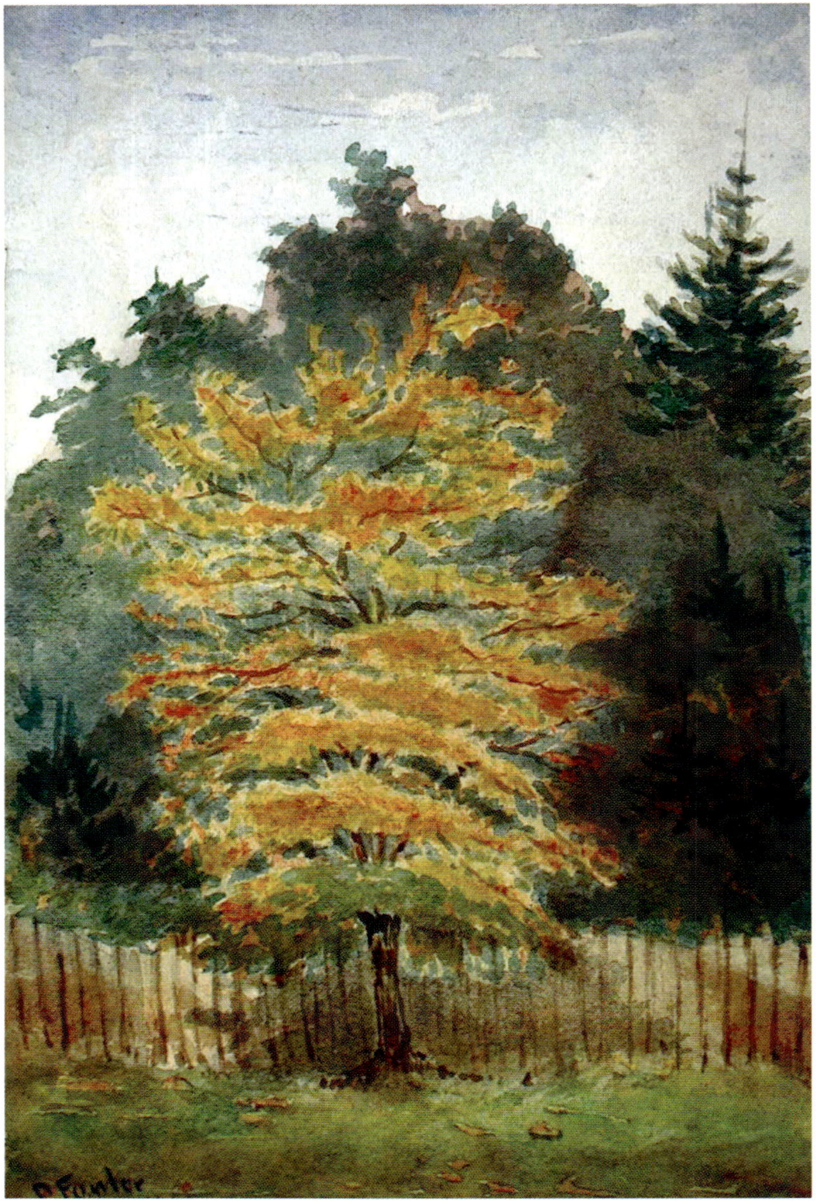

Cat. 45
Tree, 1886, AEAC

Preface and Acknowledgements

In 1979 the Agnes Etherington Art Centre organized and circulated an exhibition entitled *Daniel Fowler of Amherst Island 1810–1894*. The exhibition was the culmination of years of research by France K. Smith, then curator of the Art Centre. The catalogue that accompanied the exhibition, with its publication of Fowler's manuscript *Autobiography or Recollections of an Artist*, re-established Fowler in the public eye by providing an assessment of his work that illuminated the esteem in which he had been held in nineteenth-century Canada. Frances Smith's meticulous research papers and photographic inventory of Fowler's work are held in the Fowler Archive at the Art Centre, and form the bedrock for all studies of the artist. They are models for all of us who follow in her footsteps. Her ground-breaking work made my task a relatively easy one, and I am enormously grateful. Her earliest work on Fowler was undertaken with Ralph Allen when he was Director of the Agnes Etherington Art Centre in the 1960s, and his appreciation of the quality of Fowler's work was important.

Amherst Island lies in Lake Ontario like a mirage on the western horizon, almost within sight of the Agnes Etherington Art Centre itself. We cherish Daniel Fowler as a regional artist. His descendants happily share our appreciation of his achievements and have been helpful at all times. In particular, I would like to thank Anna Hitchins, AnnaMaria Osier, RaeAnn Osier, Leslie Turpin, Margaret Parham, and Joan Riches.

In 1992 Jean Johnstone donated previously unknown Fowler manuscripts that were found in the Fowler house on Amherst Island. These have revealed a literary side to the artist and brought new perspectives to the study of the man. Over the years, Frances K. Smith and Allison Morehead, among others, have assisted in the transcription of these manuscripts in Fowler's difficult hand. Andrea Terry undertook research and the accessioning of a large acquisition of Fowler material during winter 2004–2005.

My thanks go to Rosemarie Tovell, former curator of Canadian prints and drawings at the National Gallery of Canada, and to her volunteers, for their assistance during my visit; to Richard Hill, formerly of the Art Gallery of Ontario; and to Tobi Bruce and Kathryn Rumbold at the Art Gallery of Hamilton. I am deeply grateful to the private collectors who have generously loaned their works. Finally, my thanks go to colleagues here who have assisted me in countless ways during the preparation of this exhibition.

The exhibition has been installed by Nigel Barnett and Scott Wallis with their usual care and attention to detail. Annabel Hanson has smoothed the path in a myriad of ways. Pat Sullivan has organized all programs associated with the exhibition, while Janet Brooke has provided fundraising expertise and good advice. My gratitude goes to them all.

Dorothy Farr
Associate Director / Curator

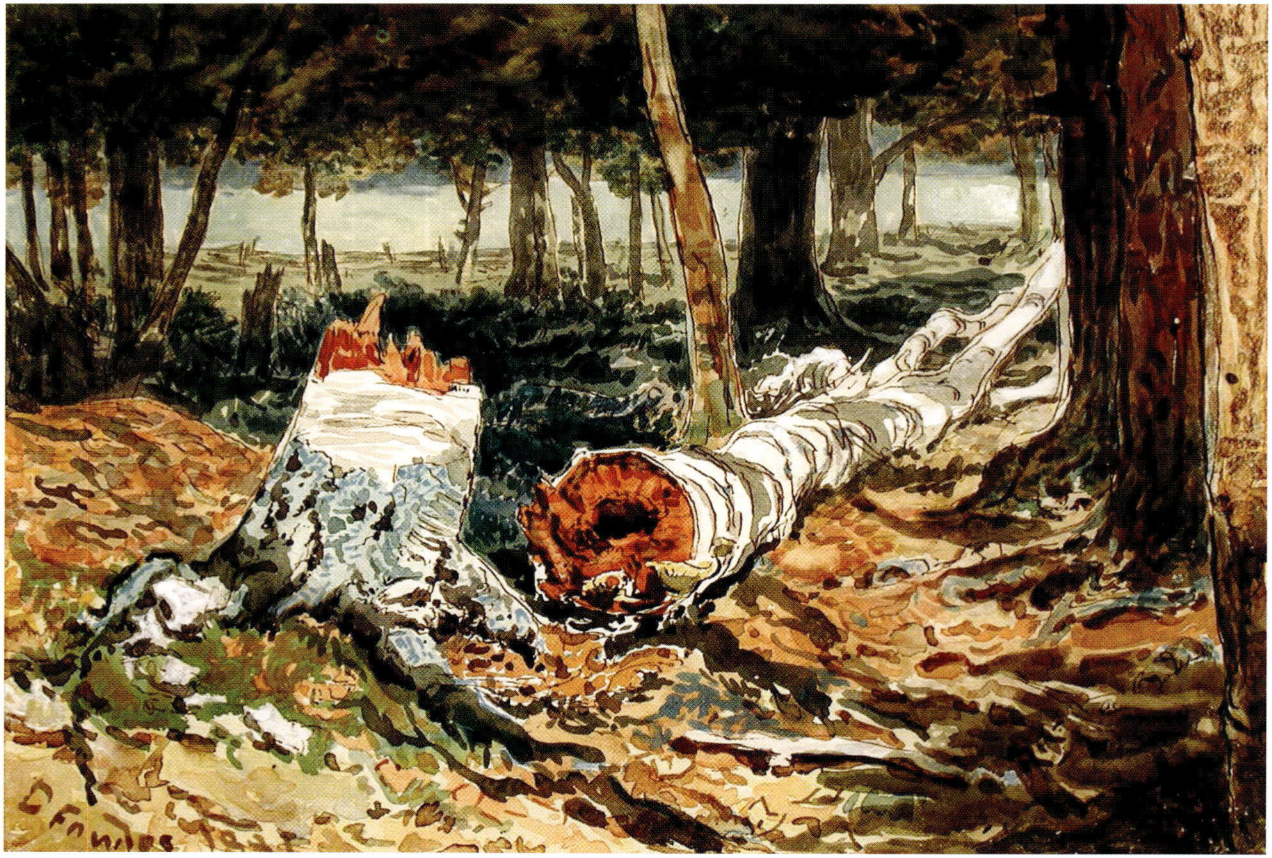

Cat. 41
Fallen Birch, 1881, AEAC

Introduction

In the latter nineteenth century, Daniel Fowler was considered "one of the fathers of Canadian art."[1] Respected by his peers and avidly collected by a circle of patrons, Fowler seemed to grow as an artist with his advancing years, rather than diminish. He was a founding member of the Ontario Society of Artists in 1872 and a charter member of the Royal Canadian Academy in 1880. In his own eyes, his crowning achievement was winning a bronze medal and diploma at the International Centennial Exhibition in Philadelphia in 1876. The medal was the only one awarded to Canada at that event, and it signified international recognition of Daniel's talents and fulfilled the daydreams of his youth. Such homage found him despite the relative isolation of his home on a farm on Amherst Island, near Kingston, Ontario.

That farm, The Cedars, was an ocean away from the genteel household in Surrey, England, into which Daniel was born in 1810. Life as a farmer would have been unthinkable in his youth, when he abandoned the study of law to take up painting; and his eminence as a Canadian artist erased the bitterness of his early, lackluster career during the 1830s as a drawing master to the titled ladies of London. In Daniel's old age, there were two achievements of which his boasted: his success as an artist and, equally, his unlikely success as a farmer. From our vantage point in the twenty-first century, Daniel Fowler's achievements may seem to belong to a vanished age. Yet in historical perspective his life was only yesterday and his track is still fresh: his paintings, his writings, his house, his descendants are with us still. The landscapes of his paintings can still be found, virtually intact, along the rural roads of Amherst Island.

Daniel Fowler's story is instructive – and instruction was on his mind in the substantial body of his writings that has survived. An autobiography he wrote in the last year of his life, together with his bequest to finance its publication, clearly indicate he wished to make his story public. (In the event, *Autobiography or Recollections of an Artist* was not published until 1979; it is abbreviated as *Autobiography* hereafter).[2] Other surviving manuscripts in Daniel's difficult hand present a variety of tales of life in Canada. A journal for the year 1863 (abbreviated as *Journal* hereafter), short articles, and some fiction that adapts events of the author's experience – all of these were intended for publication. Little made it into print in Daniel's lifetime, but his desire to reach an audience is plain. Eventually, Daniel found some success publishing occasional book reviews in Canadian magazines.

But Daniel's watercolours are of a higher order of expression and are a significant achievement. Together, his paintings and writings provide us with a uniquely detailed portrait of an artist's life in nineteenth-century Canada.

1. Unknown author [possibly Annie Rothwell Christie], obituary of Elizabeth Fowler, 1903, clipping from unknown newspaper, Fowler Archive, Agnes Etherington Art Centre (AEAC). Also *British Whig* (Kingston), 14 June 1880.

2. Smith, Frances K. *Daniel Fowler of Amherst Island 1810–1894* (Kingston: Agnes Etherington Art Centre, 1979), 81-182.

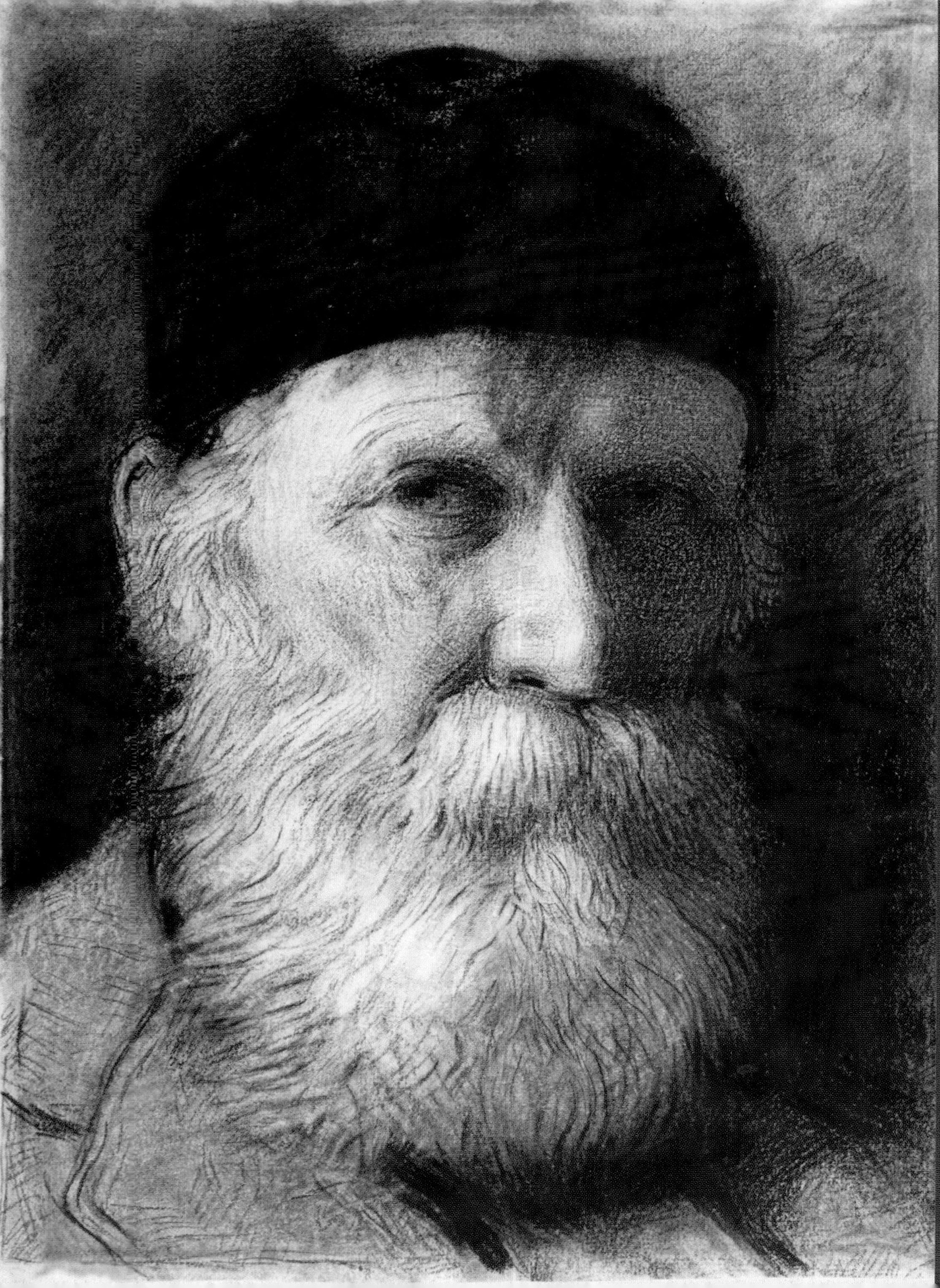

Cat. 49. *Portrait of the Artist*, around 1886, National Gallery of Canada, Ottawa

Daniel

I lived entirely out of the artist world, and could never compare notes with other painters. I deem that no disadvantage.

—Fowler, *Autobiography*, 161

Daniel

Mr. Fowler was of a kindly disposition, quiet in manner, a gentleman of the old school with perfect manners.

—J.W.H. Watts, Watts Manuscript, Scrapbook, February 1902, Montreal Museum of Fine Arts Library

Mr. Fowler was a man who loved righteousness and hated iniquity; and, moreover, [had] a good opinion of his own merits....

—J.W.L. Forster, "Early Artists of Ontario," *Canadian Magazine*, V (May/October 1895), 21

I had some very intelligent and highly cultured people on Amherst Island, old Mr. Fowler perhaps the most so.... I used to meet Mr. Fowler, though then quite old, when driving through the parish, with canvas and easel in his buggy, going to or returning from sketching.

—William Roberts, The Rectory, Adolphustown, Ontario, to unknown recipient, 24 August 1912, Queen's University Archives, Kingston

The son [Reginald Fowler] opened his eyes with amazement when I told him of his father's eminence in the world of art.

— Hector Charlesworth, *Candid Chronicles* (Toronto: Macmillan, 1925), 331

He was very tall, very thin, and very slightly made. Fair as a woman and pale, one could see at a glance that he was of very delicate health and constitution, and he told me that he had been so from his earliest childhood.... evidently a well educated man.... He was fastidious, shy, and naturally unsocial.... He preferred to have his time with a book.... He sat well in his saddle, with a light hand, and he was a good horseman. He was also an excellent driver.... There now came prominently into view [latent qualities of] industry, perseverance, calculation, economy; above all and best of all, a self-reliance; a careful and habitual following up of premises to a conclusion. [In sum, he was a] steady, sober, straightforward, industrious, persevering and not unsuccessful "gentleman settler."

—Fowler, "George Ommaney: The 'Gentleman Settler,'" 1860s, manuscript 35-18.02, Agnes Etherington Art Centre[1]

I met him once about a year before his death in 1894, a tall, patriarchal figure, the recognized doyen of Canadian painters, for though he was English by birth, he was in the fullest sense a Canadian who owed his inspiration to his Canadian surroundings.

—Hector Charlesworth, "Autobiography of a Canadian Painter," *Queen's Quarterly*, XLV, 1 (spring 1938), 88

1. This short story is a thinly disguised account of Fowler's own early years on Amherst Island.

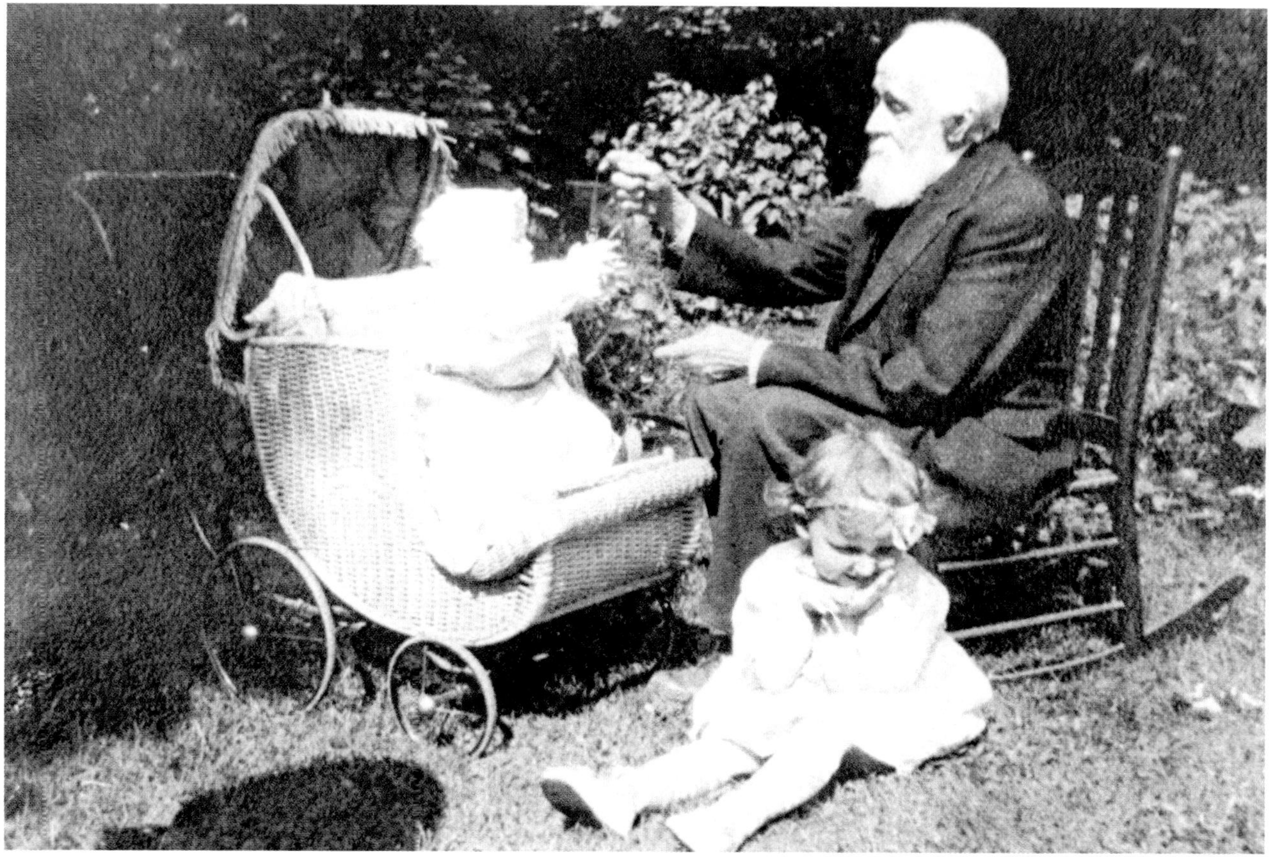

Daniel Fowler in old age, Fowler Archive, AEAC

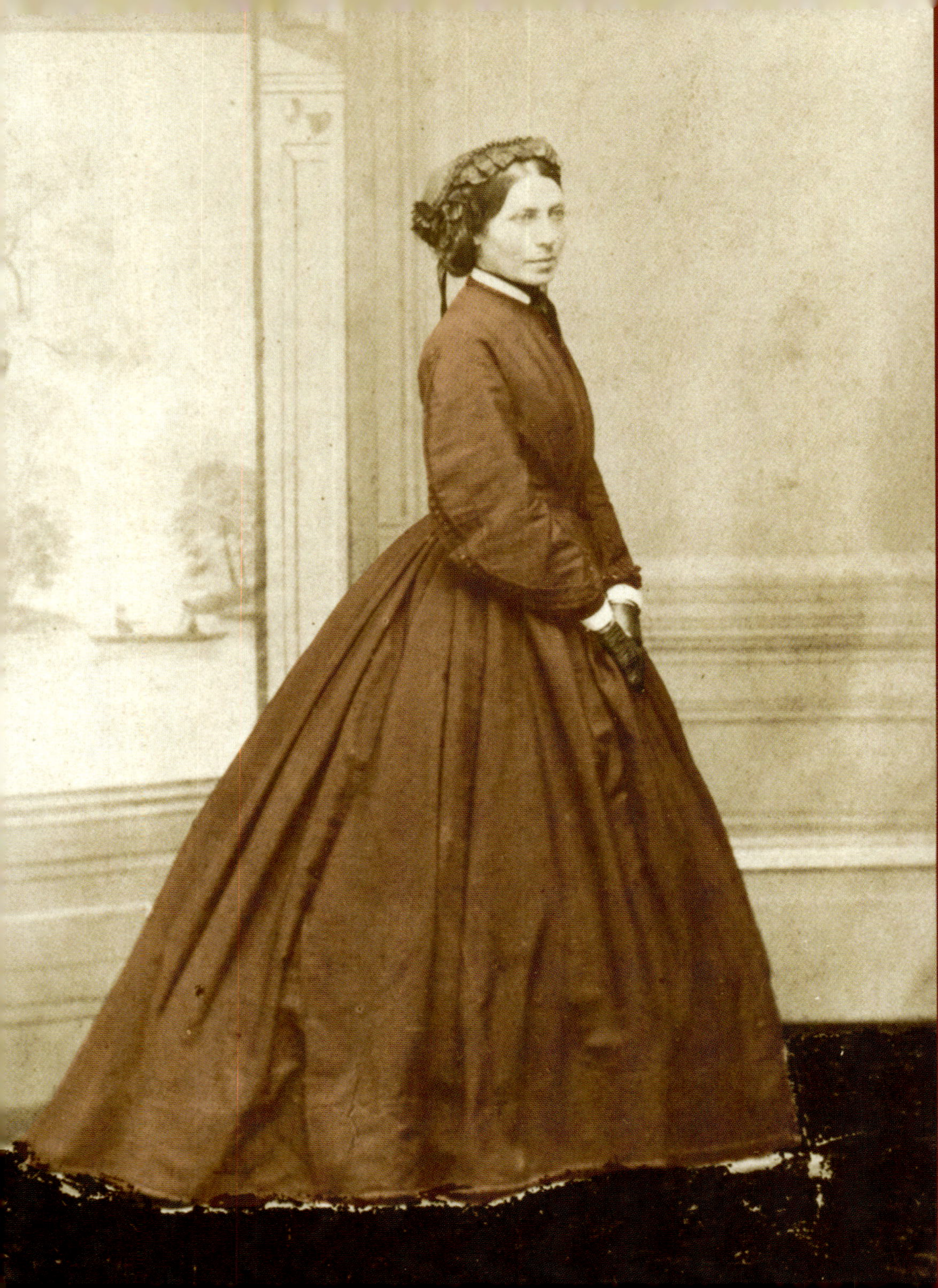

Bessy Fowler by Sheldon Photograph, Kingston, Canada West, early 1860s, ambrotype, Queen's University Archives, Kingston

Bessy

She accompanied him [Daniel] to Canada, in which country two of her five children were born. They settled at once in the year 1843 in the beautiful spot which has thus for nearly sixty years been their home, a home known far and near by those privileged to share its every ready hospitality, as the abode of culture and refinement.... As a friend and hostess, she was widely valued for a brightness of intellect that never failed to the last, and a delicate graciousness of manner and demeanour belonging perhaps more to the earlier age she so well remembered and represented than to the present day. Born in the year 1811, Mrs. Fowler had lived in the reigns of five British Sovereigns, and took a never ceasing interest in public questions of importance, as well as being a devoted lover of art and literature.

—Unknown author [possibly Annie Rothwell Christie],
obituary of Elizabeth Fowler, 1903

Bessy

In his various writings, Daniel seldom mentioned his wife Bessy, and never by name. The few descriptions of her define a dignified, intelligent, capable woman with a physical stamina greater than her husband's. Like many women of her era, she can be glimpsed only as a shadow in the background, as family housekeeper, nurse, and companion.

Daniel Fowler and Elizabeth (Bessy) Gale (1811–1903) were married at St. Pancras Church, London, on 8 August 1835. The bride was the twenty-four-year-old sister of the groom's best friend and traveling companion, Robert Leake Gale. Her mother came from a distinguished military family; her father, Thomas Gale, had been a lawyer in London. Bessy brought a considerable inheritance to the marriage in rental properties and annuities, the income from which eventually came to her following the death of her mother. It was an excellent marriage for Daniel, and he and Bessy shared life together for fifty-nine years.

Daniel and Bessy became the parents of five surviving children: Mary Ann Bessy (1837–1927), Caroline Lucy (1839–1866; her twin was stillborn), William Augustus (1840–1883), Frances Louisa (1843-1919), and Reginald Amherst (1845–1923).

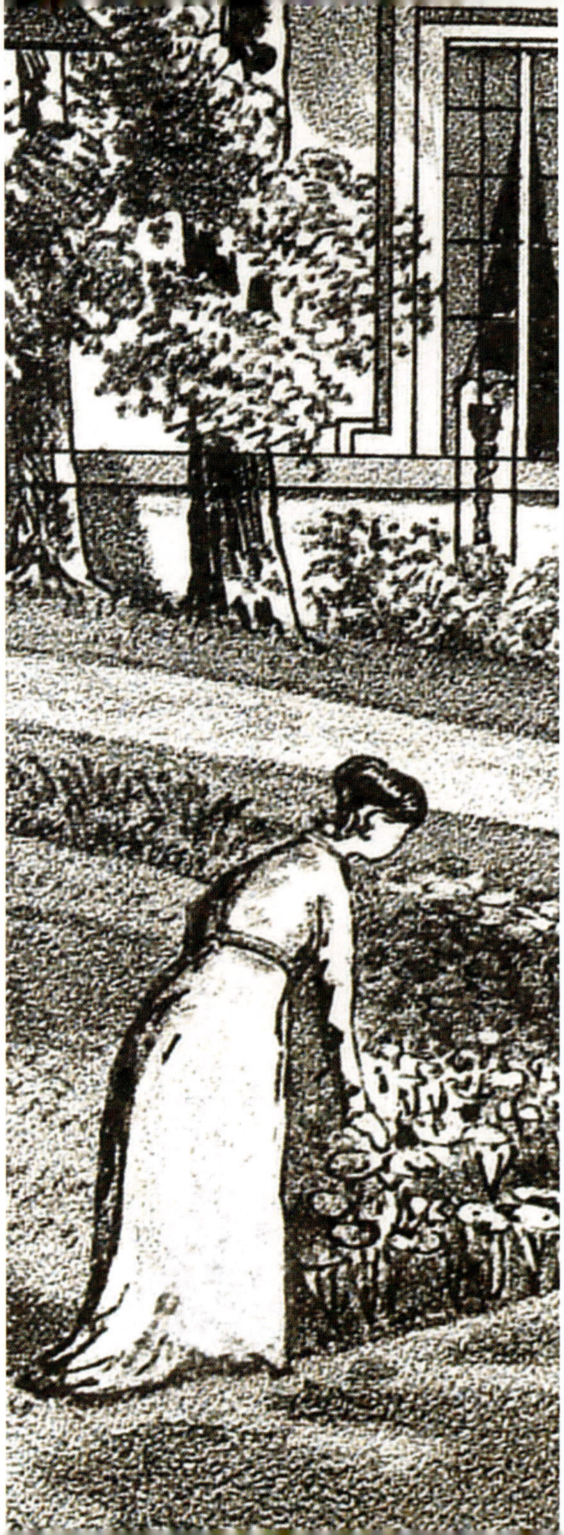

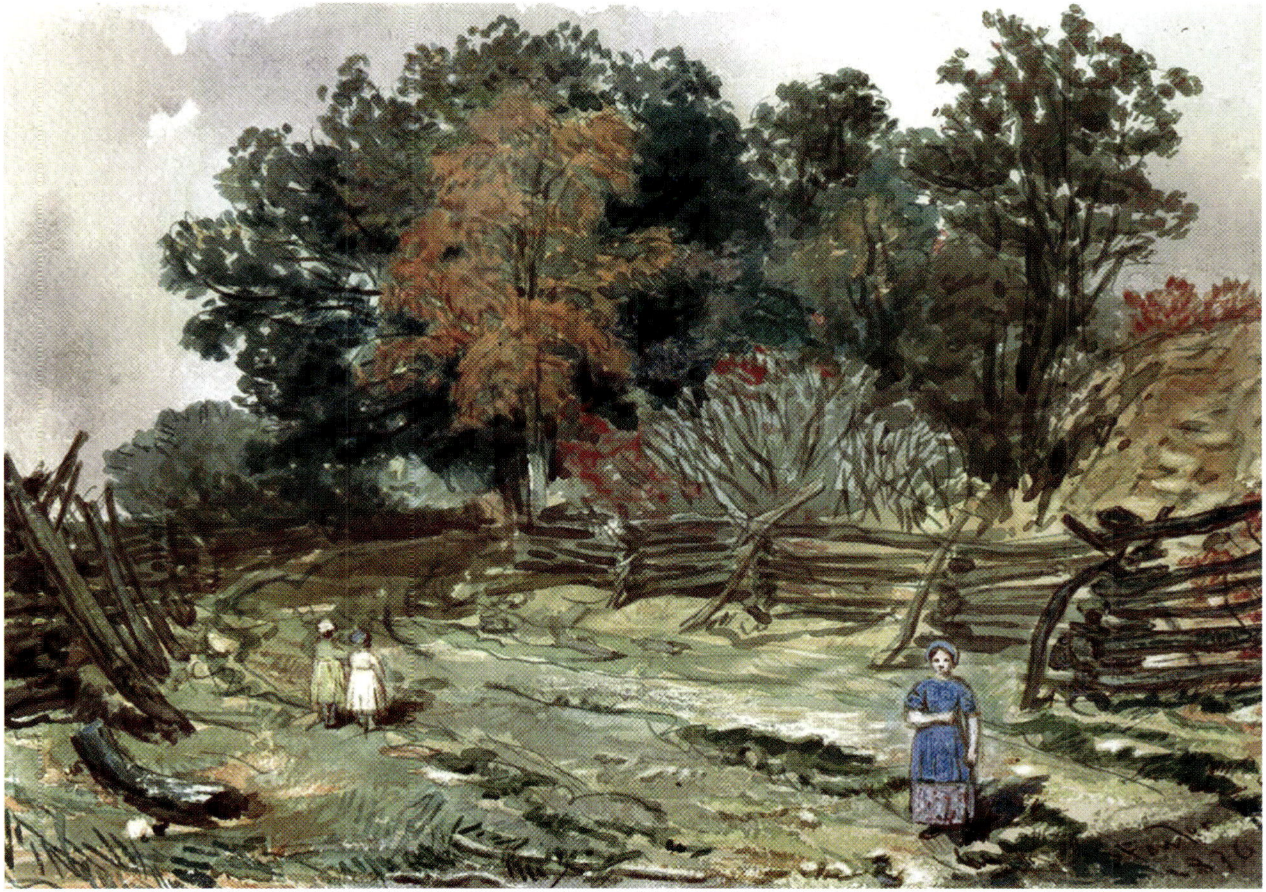

Cat. 26
Lane with Children, Amherst Island, 1876, AEAC

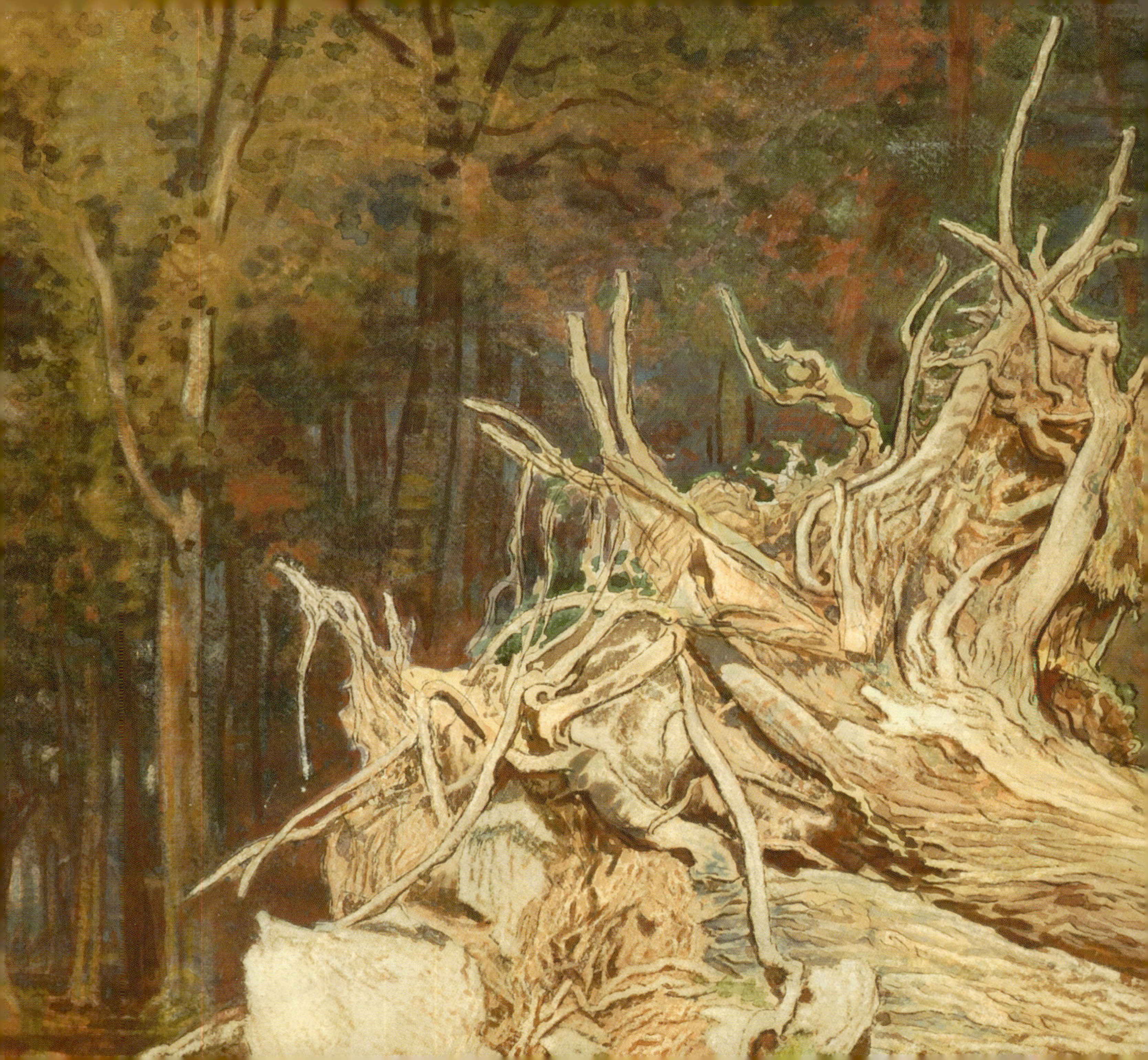

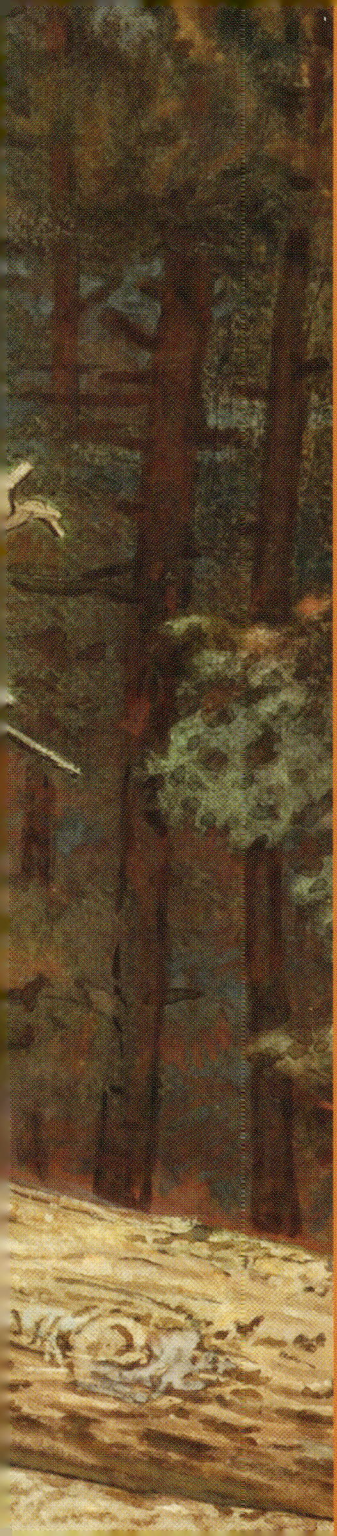

Cat. 34. *Fallen Tree*, 1880, AEAC (detail)

Before Canada

The idea of emigration came into my head. It was repulsive to me.... I had always looked upon it with a contemptuous pity. It must be a poor creature I thought for whom his dear old country did not suffice.

—Fowler, *Autobiography*, 126

Before Canada

Our knowledge of Daniel's early life comes from his *Autobiography*, written in the final year of his life. By his own account Daniel was a solitary, sensitive, bookish boy raised in the austerity of a pre-Victorian nursery and torn from the affections of his mother at the age of eight to endure the miseries of boarding-school life.

Daniel Fowler was born at Champion Hill, Surrey, on 10 February 1810, the eldest son among ten (possibly twelve) children of Daniel Fowler (1780?–1829) and Mary Ann Pope (1779/80–1860/62). He was raised in the rural, gentrified atmosphere of a Jane Austen novel[1] at Down Hall, Down (later, Downe), Kent — a property he was later quick to point out was not Down *House*, famous as the home of Charles Darwin. Down Hall was settled upon Daniel's mother by her uncle, along with a considerable income from rental properties. Daniel is silent on the subject of his father, who died in 1829 in Brussels, where family tradition has it he was avoiding British creditors. However, Daniel is effusive about his mother. They shared a love of books, and he describes himself as her "factotum."[2]

An excellent student, Daniel was put to the study of law by his father — an unwelcome scheme dropped after his father died. Daniel decided instead that he would be a painter, and moved to London in 1832 to study with the artist J. D. Harding (1798–1863). His mother's trustees provided three hundred guineas for three years' tuition and a generous living allowance. Upon Daniel's marriage in August of 1835, this allowance was increased to cover the rental of a house and the expenses of family life.

In his *Autobiography* Daniel writes in detail of a carefree year of travel, 1834–1835, which he spent sketching with his future brother-in-law, Robert Leake Gale in the Netherlands, Switzerland, and Italy. Following this formative experience, Daniel returned to marry and take up the life of a gentleman painter in London. This meant an annual sketching trip to picturesque locales, the (very) occasional display of paintings in London exhibitions, and a dreary occupation as drawing master to aristocratic but untalented ladies in London. With a growing family to support, and accumulating debts, Daniel gradually came to realize that his genteel life in London could not be sustained. Meanwhile, his health was seriously affected by the "close, smoky London streets,"[3] and his mother's fortune was dwindling as new railways drew tenants away from her ageing properties to new suburbs.

It was with humiliation and anguish that Daniel forced himself to the realization that in order to support his family independently, he must give up his career as an artist and leave England for a colony where he might regain his health and fortune. In this he was not alone. Some eleven million people crossed the Atlantic from the British Isles between 1780 and 1890, in the largest migration in history.[4] Those with Daniel's background were the least likely to succeed. Generally, the gentry lacked the necessary will and stamina for success in the colonies.[5] Daniel's brother-in-law Robert Gale had already left for British North America (the future Canada) and was living on a farm on Amherst Island, Canada West (the future Ontario), so in spring 1843 Daniel followed him. Daniel had no experience as a farmer, was in delicate health, and had a family of three small children and a pregnant wife.

With typical resolve Daniel read extensively on the subject of emigration from a growing list of books available on the subject.[6] He had an allowance from his mother to sustain

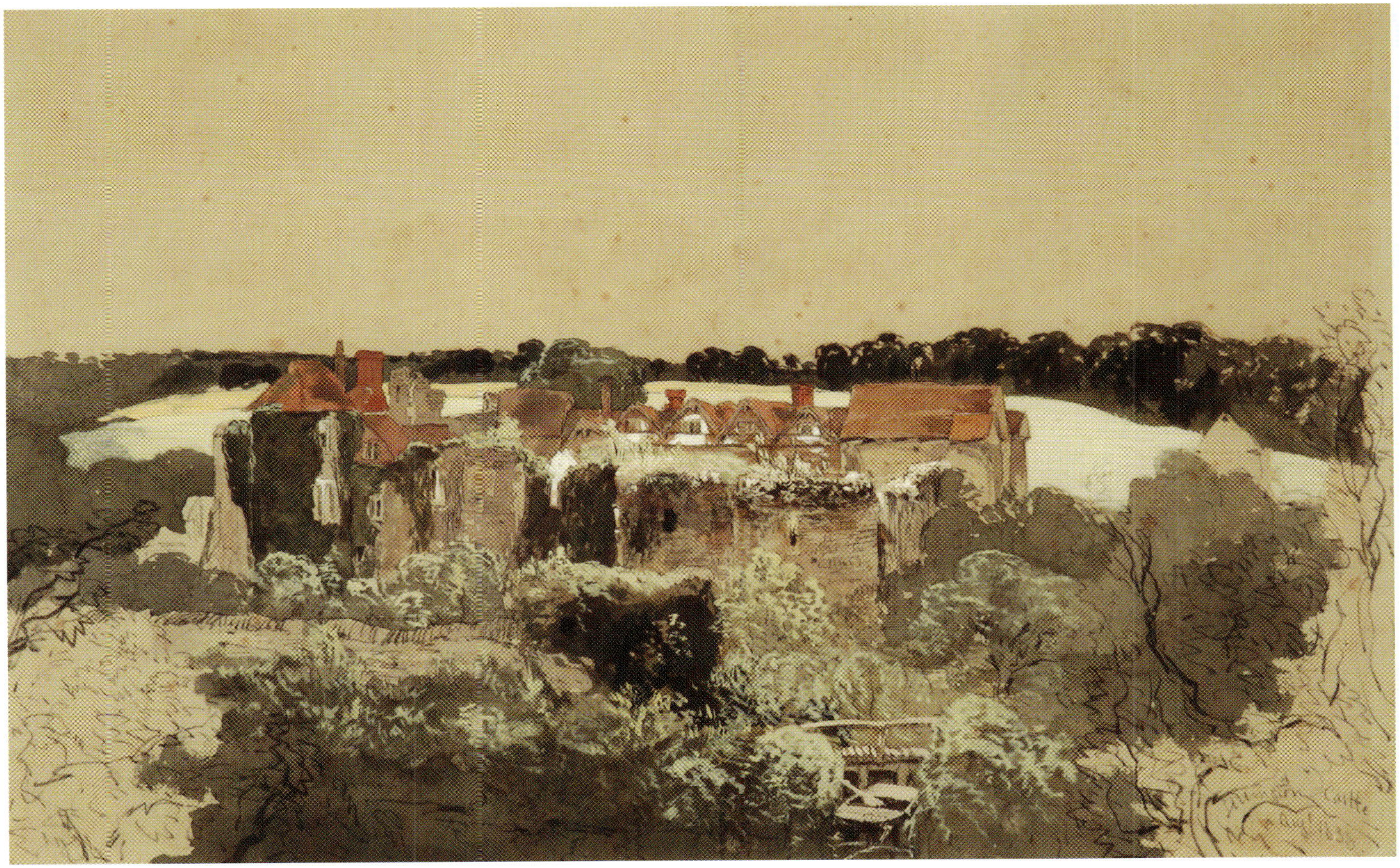

Cat. 1
Allington Castle, 1838, AEAC

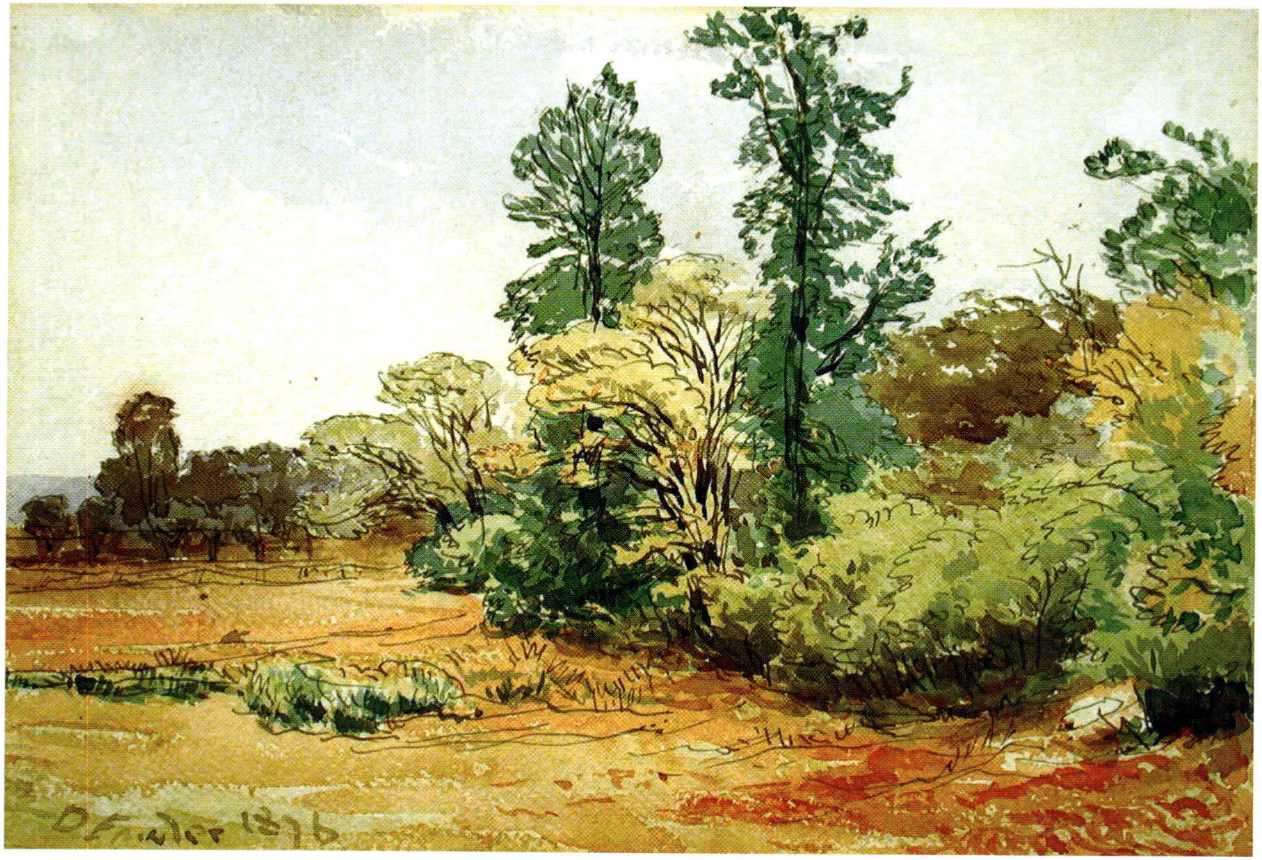

Cat. 25
Spring at Adolphustown, 1876, AEAC

the expenses of the voyage and the purchase of a farm, although he hoped in a few years to become independent. He enlisted his younger brother Reginald to accompany and assist his family on the journey. Having done his homework, Daniel booked passage as recommended by the experts, choosing the shorter and more comfortable passage aboard an American packet steamer bound for New York City, rather than the longer, rougher passage aboard a British packet bound for Quebec City. He chose early summer, when the Atlantic is relatively calm; hired a children's nurse to accompany them on the crossing; and insisted that a female steward be engaged because his wife Bessy would otherwise be the only "lady" on board and might require personal assistance.[7] They arrived safely in New York after twenty-eight days at sea. A short trip from New York City to Oswego upstate, and then across Lake Ontario, brought the Fowler family to Kingston, and the next day to Robert Gale's farm on Amherst Island, Canada West.

1. Austen's *Sense and Sensibility* was published in 1811, the year following Daniel's birth.
2. *Autobiography*, 95.
3. *Autobiography*, 99. In the five years following Daniel's father's death, five of Daniel's siblings died, probably of consumption (tuberculosis), the pandemic of its era. Daniel may have also suffered from the disease, or from asthma. In 1866, his daughter Carry died of tuberculosis.
4. Edwin C. Guillet, *The Great Migration* (Toronto: University of Toronto Press, 1963), vii.
5. Reginald Fowler, who was Daniel's brother and accompanied Daniel and Bessy during their first year in Canada, wrote: "It was undoubtedly an act of folly, to endeavour to sustain, in such a country as Canada, the life of pleasure to which most of them [gentlemen settlers, including Daniel Fowler's brother-in-law Robert Gale] had been accustomed at home. Still only those who have been put to the test, know how difficult a thing it is to abandon at once deeply-rooted habits and feelings: to work instead of play" (*Hither and Thither* [London: Frederick R. Daldy, 1854], 226).
6. The list of possibilities is extensive for books on settlement in North America written during the 1830s and early 1840s. A Fowler manuscript entitled " 'A' Books upon Canada" (manuscript 35.018.22, Agnes Etherington Art Centre) provides Fowler's abbreviations for a few of the books he consulted. "Backwoods" may be Catherine Parr Traill's *The Backwoods of Canada*, published in 1836; "Letters" is almost certainly Thomas Radcliff's *Authentic Letters from Upper Canada*, first published in 1833, because Daniel was aware that he was about to become a neighbour of Radcliff's son on Amherst Island; "Bonnycastle" refers to Sir Richard Bonnycastle's *The Canadas in 1841* published in London in 1841–1842; "Canadas" may refer to Andrew Picken's *The Canadas, as they at present commend themselves to the enterprise of emigrants, colonists and capitalists*, published in London in 1832.
7. Bessy was seasick for much of the voyage (*Autobiography*, 127).

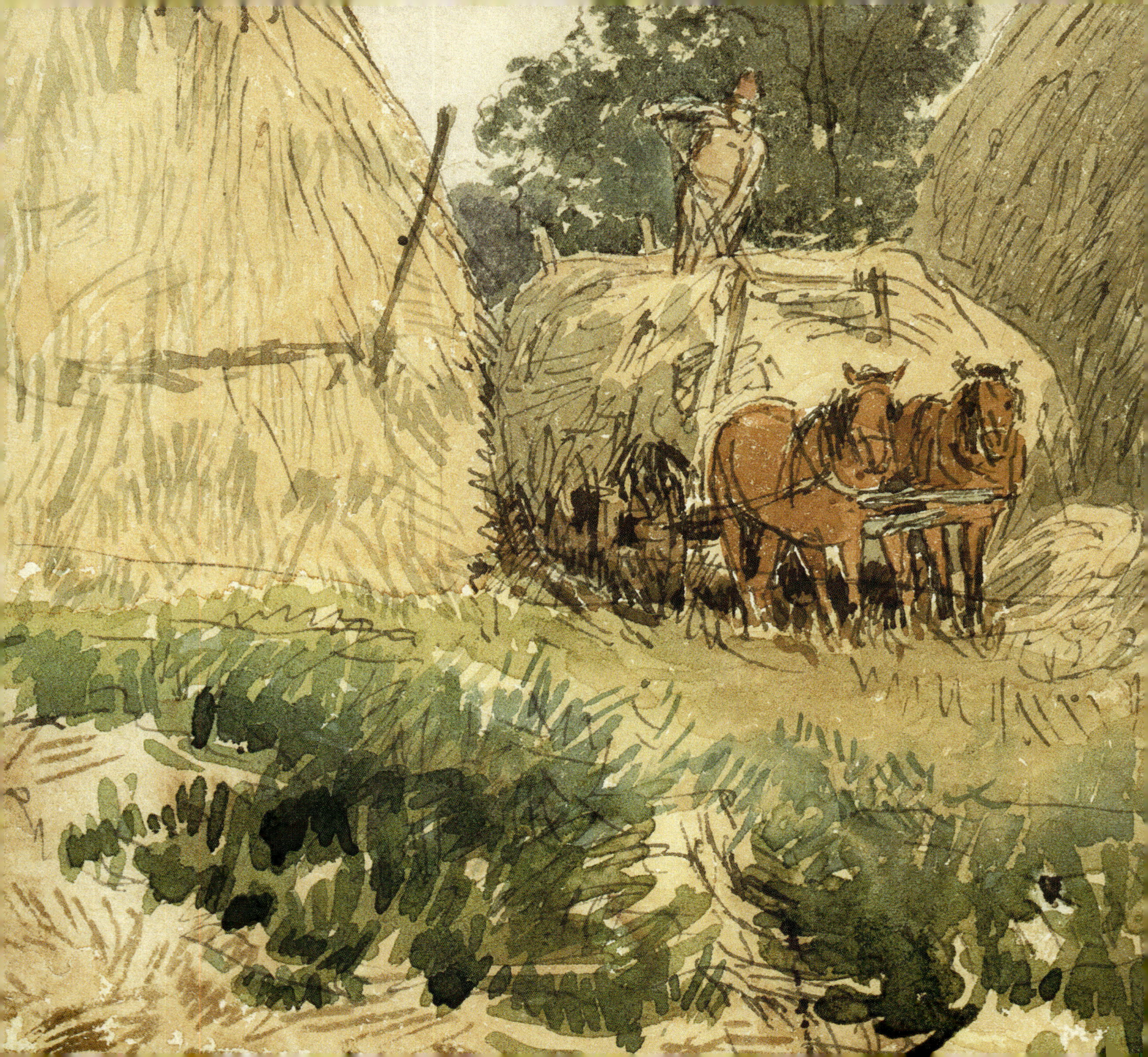

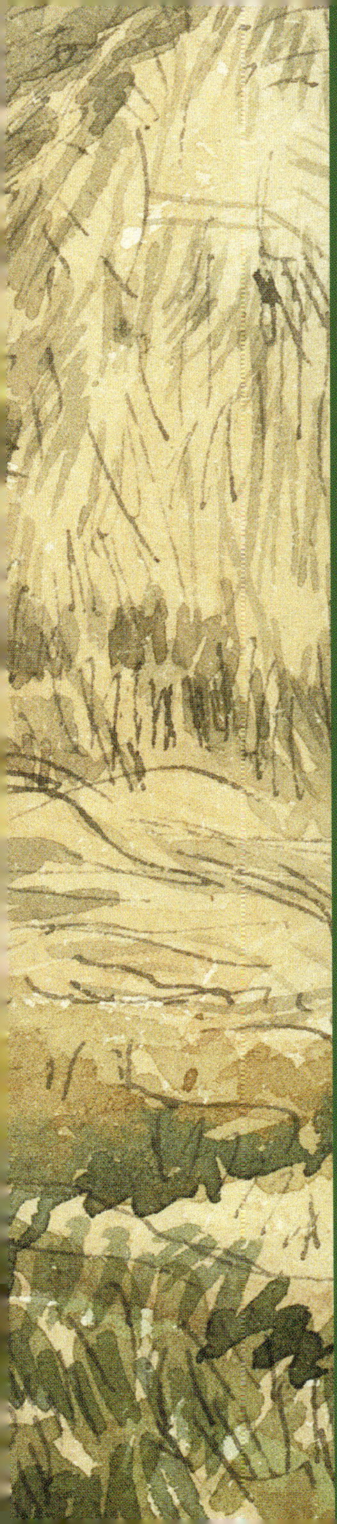

Cat. 14. *Haymaking, Amherst Island*, 1875, AEAC (detail)

Amherst Island

Whatever my life may have been worth,
I most assuredly owe it to Amherst Island.

—Fowler, *Autobiography*, 128

Amherst Island

Comprising some 16,500 acres in area, Amherst Island lies just west of Kingston, off the north shore of Lake Ontario at its eastern end. When Daniel arrived in early summer 1843, there was a steamer service between the island and Kingston, a city then basking in fleeting glory as capital of the United Canadas. British imperial forces were stationed at Kingston; Queen's College (now Queen's University) had been founded there in 1841. To Daniel, Amherst Island would have looked like a rural haven nestled close to a bustling urban centre of colonial power.

A large tract at the eastern end of Amherst Island was owned by an absentee Irish landlord, Lord Mountcashel. That tract, with its many rented farms, was poorly maintained; and the stream of destitute, ill-prepared Irish immigrants dumped onto it by the profiteering Mountcashel was a continuing source of concern.[1] Daniel's initial view of the island, while traveling to Bessy's brother's farm, was depressing:

> Emerging into the open country, no more beauty greeted us. Here the features were a shabby ill-made road, bounded by the hideous snake fences, from which there is never a moment's respite; half cleared up fields and ruinably poor buildings.[2]

However, the western end of the island had been settled by United Empire Loyalists in the late eighteenth century. Here Daniel found:

> The last half dozen places had thriving orchards of apple trees in full blossom. The houses and barns too were better, the fields better cleared, and there was not quite so much of the untidiness and disorder.... [W]e passed through a most beautiful piece of road, skirting the water of the bay of Quinte... and bounded on either side by a luxuriant growth of cedars....[3]

It was here that Daniel purchased his beloved farm The Cedars. This property of 100 acres included some picturesque woods surrounding the house, which would be useful for sheltering cattle and would eventually supply the subject-matter for many watercolours. "For fifty years, it has been my favourite haunt," Daniel later declared.[4] He purchased the farm literally lock, stock, and barrel for £500.

> The exhilaration of the air was matchless. Already I was feeling new life stirring within me as I drew my breath....[5] Climate decidedly good on the whole; hard and long winter, but a superb summer, a summer of fire flies, humming birds, and Indian corn.[6]

At The Cedars Daniel commenced his new career as a gentleman farmer by observing and helping his hired man, taking notes as he went. All was well until a bright December morning in 1847 when the house caught fire. While his wife and young children huddled nearby, Daniel and his neighbours dragged belongings from the burning house. But the house and much of its contents were lost. After seeing his family to shelter, Daniel walked alone in the night to the site of the charred ruins and wept.[7] Not long before, Daniel had returned to his mother the allowance that she had provided him. Now, suddenly, his family was homeless, his assets diminished, and

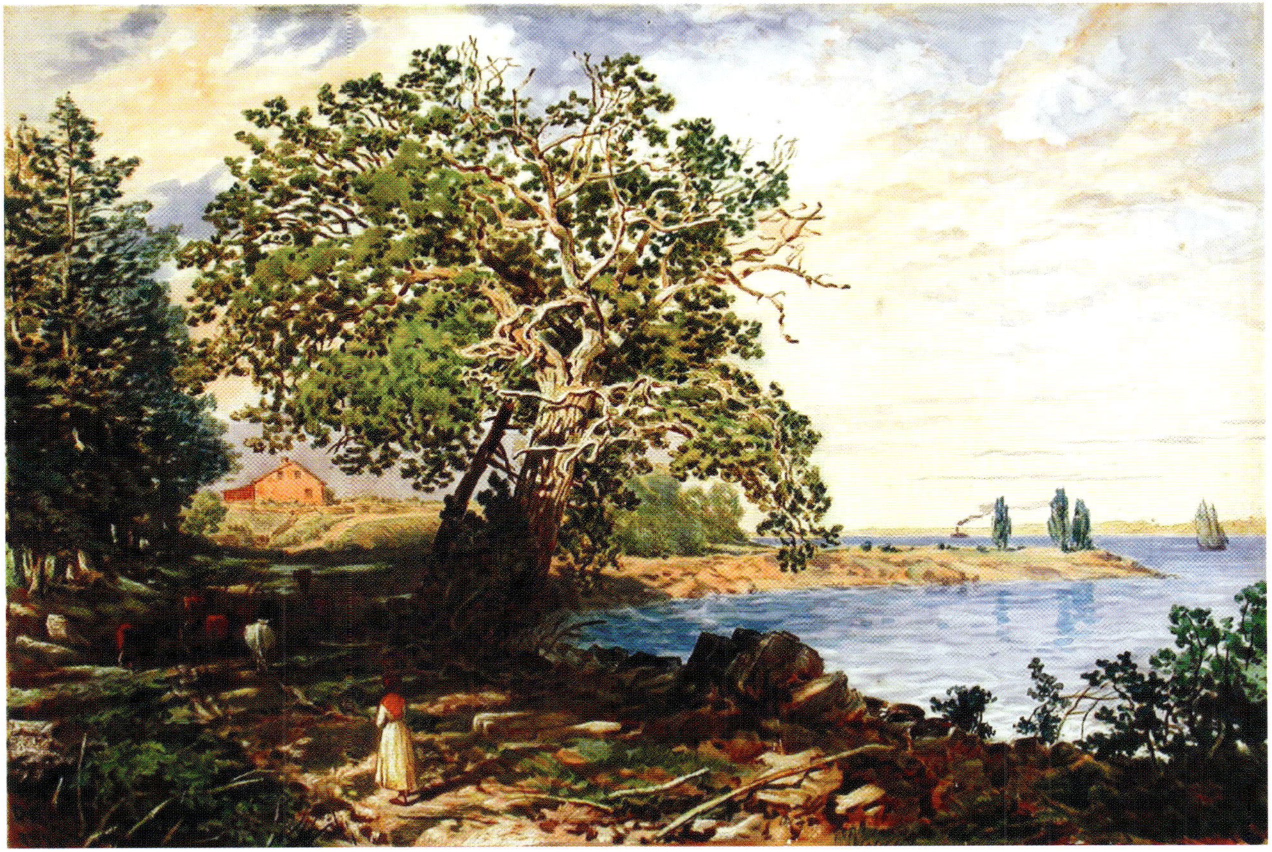

Cat. 15
Sunset on Amherst Island, 1875, AEAC

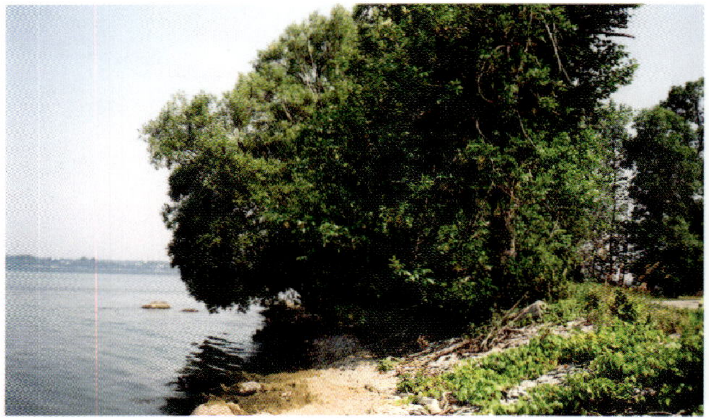

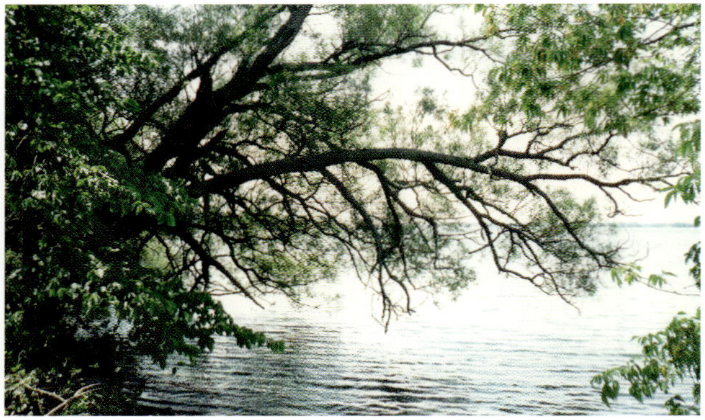

many essentials lost in the fire. It was a turning point in his life.

The next day he began again. The house was rebuilt in two phases, the initial log structure largely by Daniel's own hands. There began a long period of grinding perseverance when for ten years he was a farmer in earnest. Although physically delicate, Daniel mastered the labour of farming without any hired men[8] and lightened his load by letting some of his acreage in shares. Gradually, as his sons grew older and could assist with work on the farm, Daniel's financial security was restored. Daniel considered his transformation from sickly gentleman artist to successful Canadian farmer to be one of the great achievements of his life:

> This morning, as it was usual, I got up at about 5, and had breakfast and was out in the field at work, a few minutes after 6, having done some few chores before breakfast. I sowed steadily, with about half an hour's rest or less, 'til 12 o'clock. Sowing consists of walking in coarse heavy boots over rough ground, to which you can pay little attention, having to attend to your cast, with a regular action of the legs and the right arm, and a pail slung round your neck, which, when it is full of peas, or wheat, weighs about 20 lbs. In the afternoon, I was on my legs again for more than 2 hours; and, tomorrow, I expect to have much the same day's work. This is pretty severe work for a man of 53, who is pretty well past work, and I record it, to show what a Canadian farmer must be prepared to do, should occasion require.[9]

1. *Journal*, 17 September 1863, manuscript 35-018.18, Agnes Etherington Art Centre (AEAC).
2. *Autobiography*, 127.
3. *Autobiography*, 128.
4. *Autobiography*, 129.
5. *Autobiography*, 127.
6. *Autobiography*, 130.
7. Daniel was quick to assert that this was the only time he succumbed to his emotions (*Autobiography*, 146).
8. Additional help was required at harvest time, but giving up a regular hired man saved money. It also saved face. As Fowler wrote in his short story "George Ommaney: The 'Gentleman Settler,'": "I will not slander women so much as to suppose that they can think it any hardship or degradation to wait upon their own husbands and children; but, when it comes to waiting upon hired laborers, it is a very different thing. I have always felt for ladies, when I have seen them so situated, sometimes with two or three men; and I never could get rid of a feeling of shame, when it occurred under my own roof" (manuscript 35-018.02, AEAC).
9. *Journal*, 24–29 April 1863.

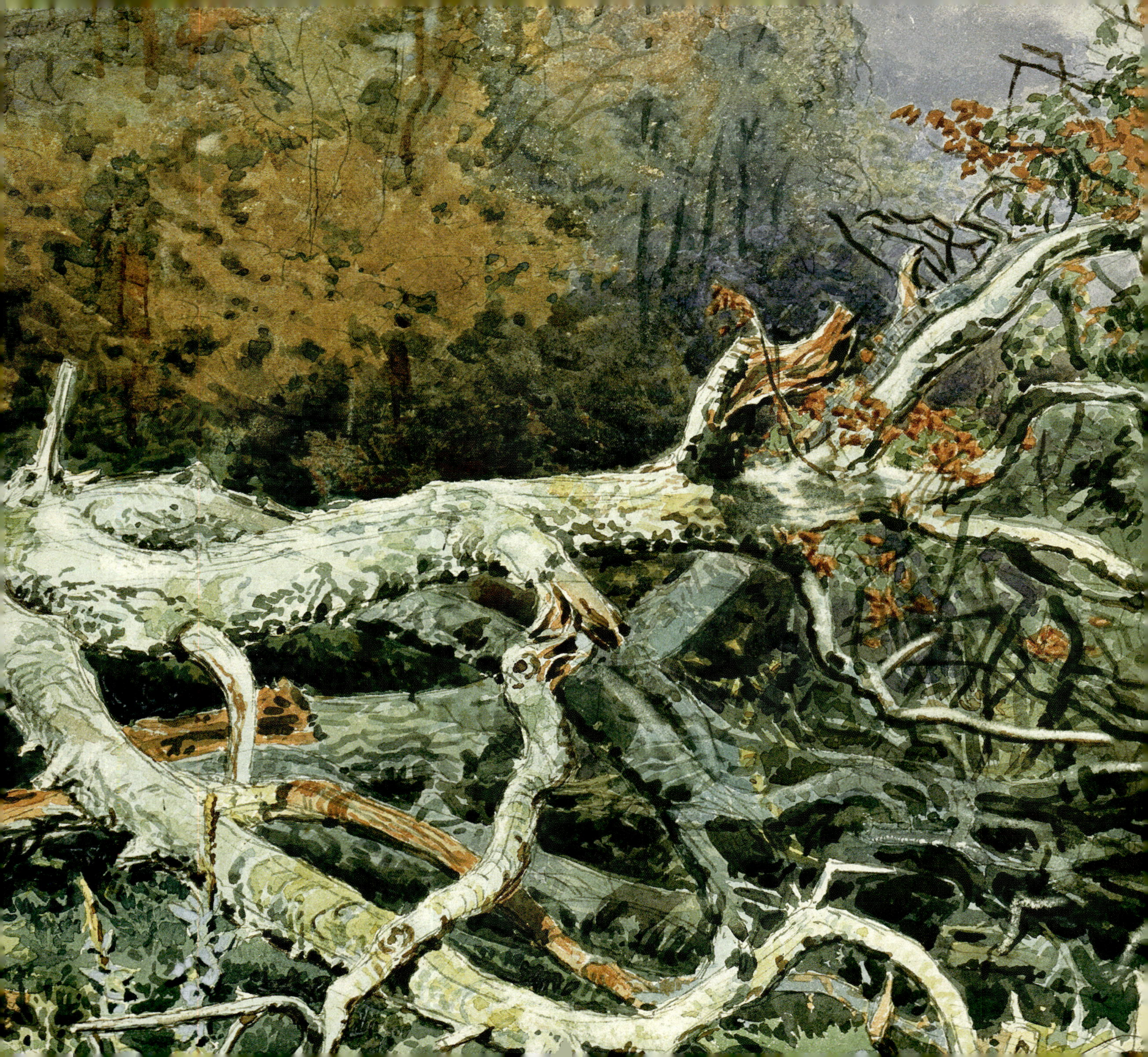

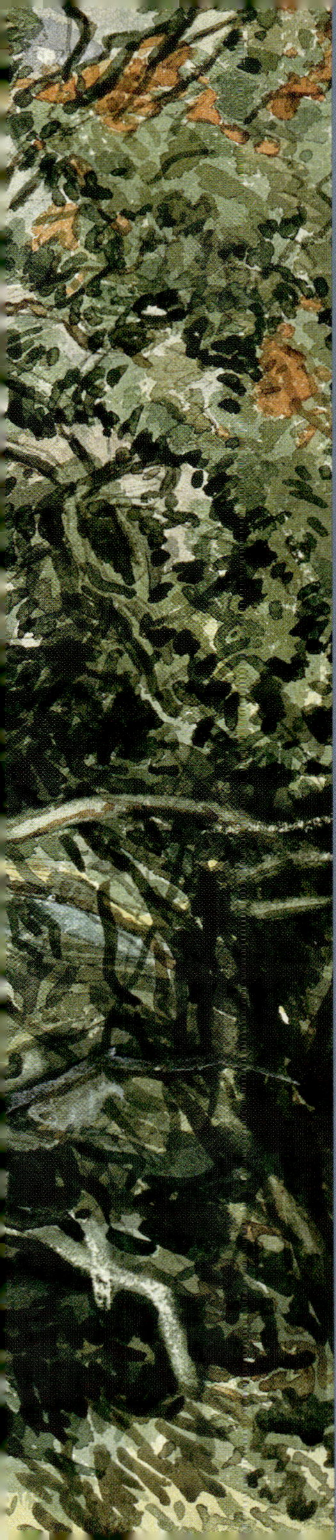

Cat. 30. *Woodland Scene*, 1878, AEAC (detail)

Daniel as Artist: an Assessment

On the whole then, I was an artist after all.... The delight that I found in my new life – my second and inner life – my profound gratification and gratitude, may be more easily imagined than described.

—Fowler, *Autobiography*, 161

Daniel as Artist: an Assessment

In 1857 Daniel returned to England to visit his mother, carrying with him a sketch of his house as a gift to her — his first painting in fourteen years. It was sufficiently admired, even by his old teacher James D. Harding, that Daniel decided to purchase some painting supplies to take back to Canada.

During his English visit, Daniel attended Royal Academy and other exhibitions in London that renewed his enthusiasm for painting. On display at the Goupil Gallery in New Bond Street was the magnificent *The Horse Fair* by Rosa Bonheur (1822–1899), which Daniel described as being "full of sunshine and daylight, as well as of life and action, fine drawing and true color."[1] These were qualities he would seek in his own work.

Daniel's portfolio of early sketches had survived the fire that destroyed his house in 1847. For two years after his return to Canada, he copied his old, monochrome European sketches, and added colour tentatively from memory. It was a recreation undertaken as time allowed, and with increasing dedication as his sons gradually relieved him of the heavier farm labour. In his studies with Harding in the 1830s, Daniel had drawn anatomical and other sketches in Harding's studio, but he had never studied colour *in situ* in a landscape setting. He came to see this as a mistake: "He [Harding] should have made me study from nature in colour, out of doors, at all possible seasons, as the fountain head, and the only one, from which true knowledge can be obtained...."[2] In 1859–1860 Daniel returned to England with his new paintings, but he found no encouragement from Harding, or from dealers in London.

Daniel knew of the youthful Pre-Raphaelite movement that was re-energizing the traditions of British painting. While in London in 1860, he viewed *The Finding of the Saviour in the Temple* by the Pre-Raphaelite William Holman Hunt (1827–1910), which he pronounced "one of the finest, if not the very finest picture yet painted by an English artist."[3] Seeing this and other Pre-Raphaelite paintings did not make Daniel a Pre-Raphaelite, yet he took inspiration from them. Wisely avoiding the Pre-Raphaelites' preference for narrative subjects, he noted their interest in depicting the "truth" of nature, and in painting outdoors in sunlight. Their experiments with white-primed canvases, which gave vibrancy to colour, would have resonated for a watercolourist who had frequently worked on white paper. In old age, Daniel wrote:

> They maintained... that purity, simplicity, and above all truth, had been lost sight of and conventionality, absurdity and falsity taken their place; that the modern painter drew his inspiration from art, or rather artificiality, and not from nature... they wanted local and actual truth.... There is something fine and grand in this creed.[4]

Sensitized by the Pre-Raphaelite Brotherhood, Daniel followed its influence through reviews in British and Canadian periodicals.[5] On his return to Canada, he began again, quite differently.

Prior to Daniel's departure for England, a neighbour had shot an owl and given it to Daniel to sketch. On his return to Amherst Island, Daniel studied the sketch he had made carefully and "knocked the background about without mercy, for I knew there was nothing I could spoil."[6] The result set him on a new path. He began to sketch from nature, learning to express himself in colour *en plein air*. Shedding the conventions

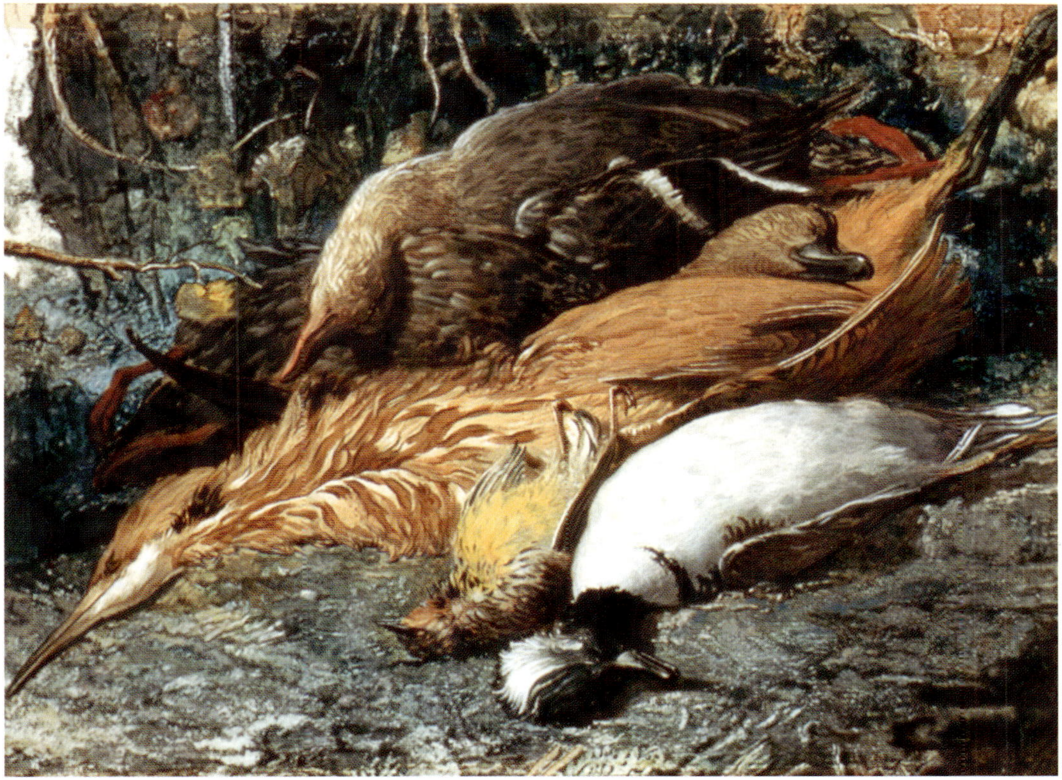

Cat. 33
Dead Canadian Game, 1879, National Gallery of Canada, Ottawa

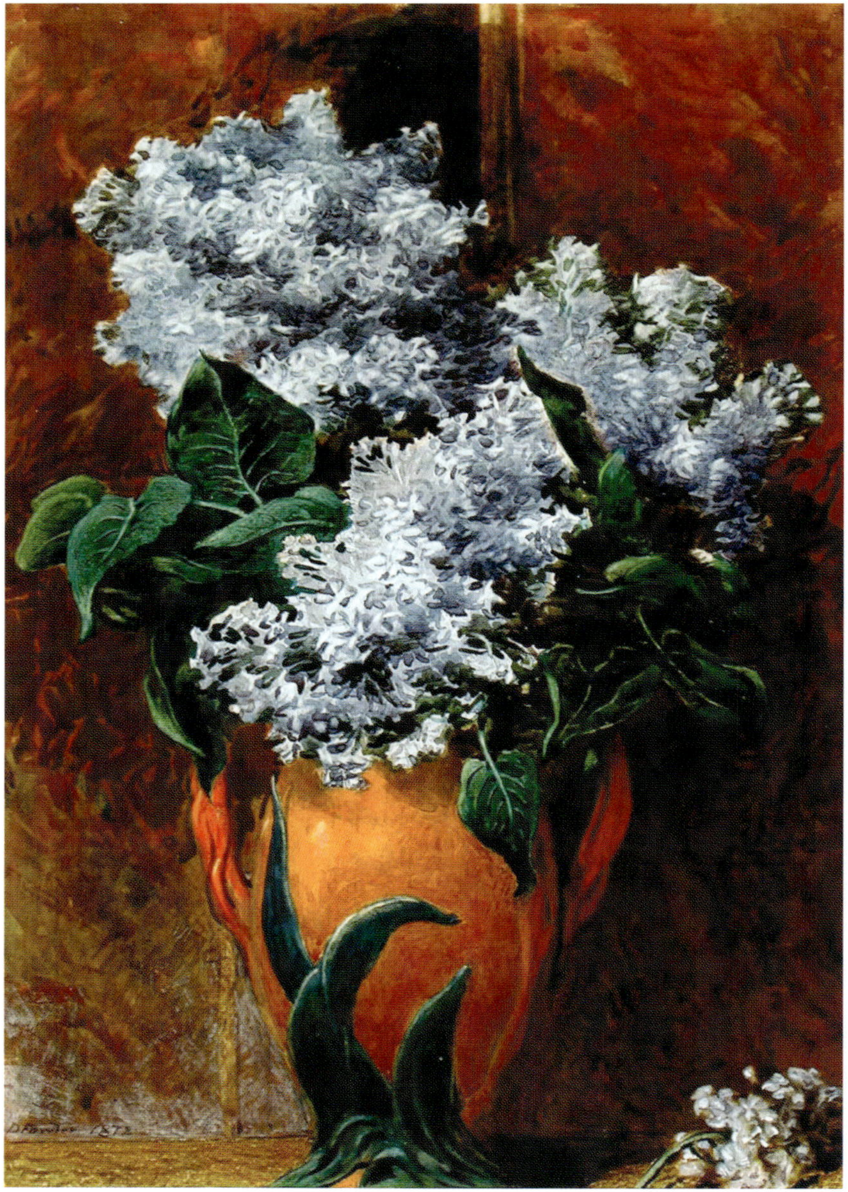

Cat. 10
Lilacs (Flower Study), 1872, AEAC

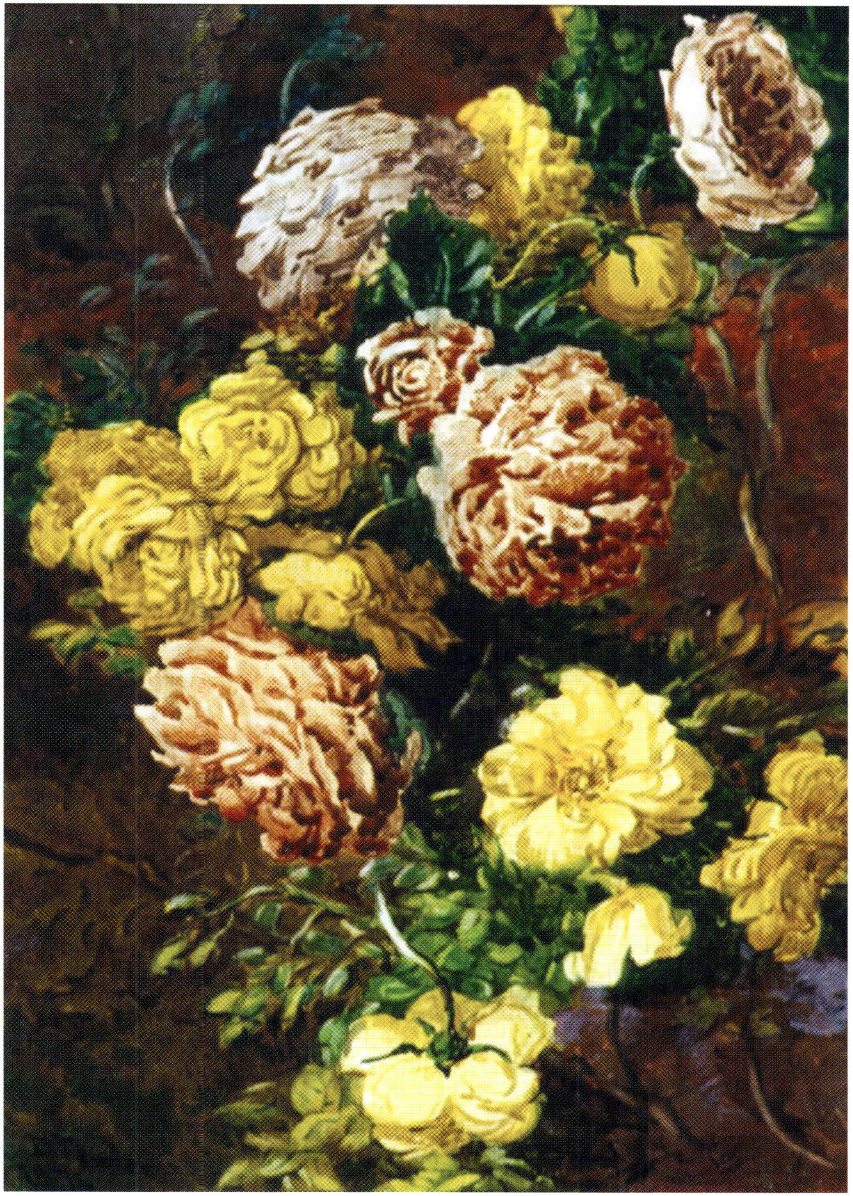

Cat. 13
Flowers, 1874, AEAC

of his early training, Daniel ventured outside into the intensity of summer sunlight to discover the secrets of rendering the light and colour of the Ontario landscape. Finally, in 1863, Daniel submitted his first works, eleven of them, for exhibition in the amateur list at the Provincial Exhibition held that year in Kingston. To his delight, he won seven prizes and pocketed $34.00 in prize money. He also made the acquaintance of William Cresswell (1822–1888), another British watercolourist who had settled in Canada (at Seaforth, Ontario), and through Cresswell began to make contact with the fragile network of artists, art exhibitions, and organizations then taking root in Canada.

Daniel continued to submit work as an amateur to the annual Provincial Exhibitions that were held at various locations – until in 1865, at London, Ontario, he dominated the amateur category so completely that the following year he was moved to the professional list.[7] Beginning in 1867, Daniel exhibited regularly at the Art Association of Montreal; in 1868 with the Society of Canadian Artists; and in 1868/69 with the American Society of Painters in Water Color. In 1872 he became a founding member of the Ontario Society of Artists. In 1880 he was invited to become a charter member of the Royal Canadian Academy, one of only twelve to be honoured. It was recognition of the esteem in which Daniel was held by his peers. In his own mind, the apex of his career was the winning of a bronze medal at the Centennial Exhibition in Philadelphia in 1876, an occasion that provided tangible evidence of international recognition. He was included in the Canadian section of the Colonial and Indian Exhibition in London, England, in 1886, and in the Canadian section of the World's Columbian Exhibition in Chicago in 1893; but by this time he was the acknowledged doyen of Canadian watercolourists.

It is instructive to examine the exhibition lists of artists' organizations, which at the time were a Canadian painter's only regular venues for public exhibition. In the early years Daniel's submissions were predominantly flower paintings and images of dead game. These were favourites with his audience, and he won renown for the technique of his backgrounds, which he had developed so fruitfully with that dead owl in 1860. European and British views are also numerous, all of them worked up from old sketches.[8] It was only gradually that regional Canadian landscapes became a major component of his exhibited work. His watercolours selected for the Colonial and Indian Exhibition of 1886 were entirely of Canadian flowers and game. (Nine of the ten were loaned by Daniel's dealer, James Spooner of Toronto, who made the selection.) However, such subjects diminished thereafter because the elderly Daniel lacked the stamina to paint rapidly before flowers died and dead game decomposed.[9] In the last years of his life Canadian landscapes dominated his subject matter.

Daniel's contemporaries particularly admired his depictions of flowers and game. *Dead Canadian Game* (cat. 33), for example, was Daniel's diploma picture, deposited with the Royal Canadian Academy when he was elected a charter member in 1880, and therefore, one assumes, highly regarded. It is a technical tour de force – the slumped weight of the dead birds spilling forward toward the viewer; the modulated tones of delicate feathers lying against the densely rich colour and boldly scraped highlights of dry earth.

Watercolour is a difficult medium to control. Working with water and pigment on paper, an artist may by error make

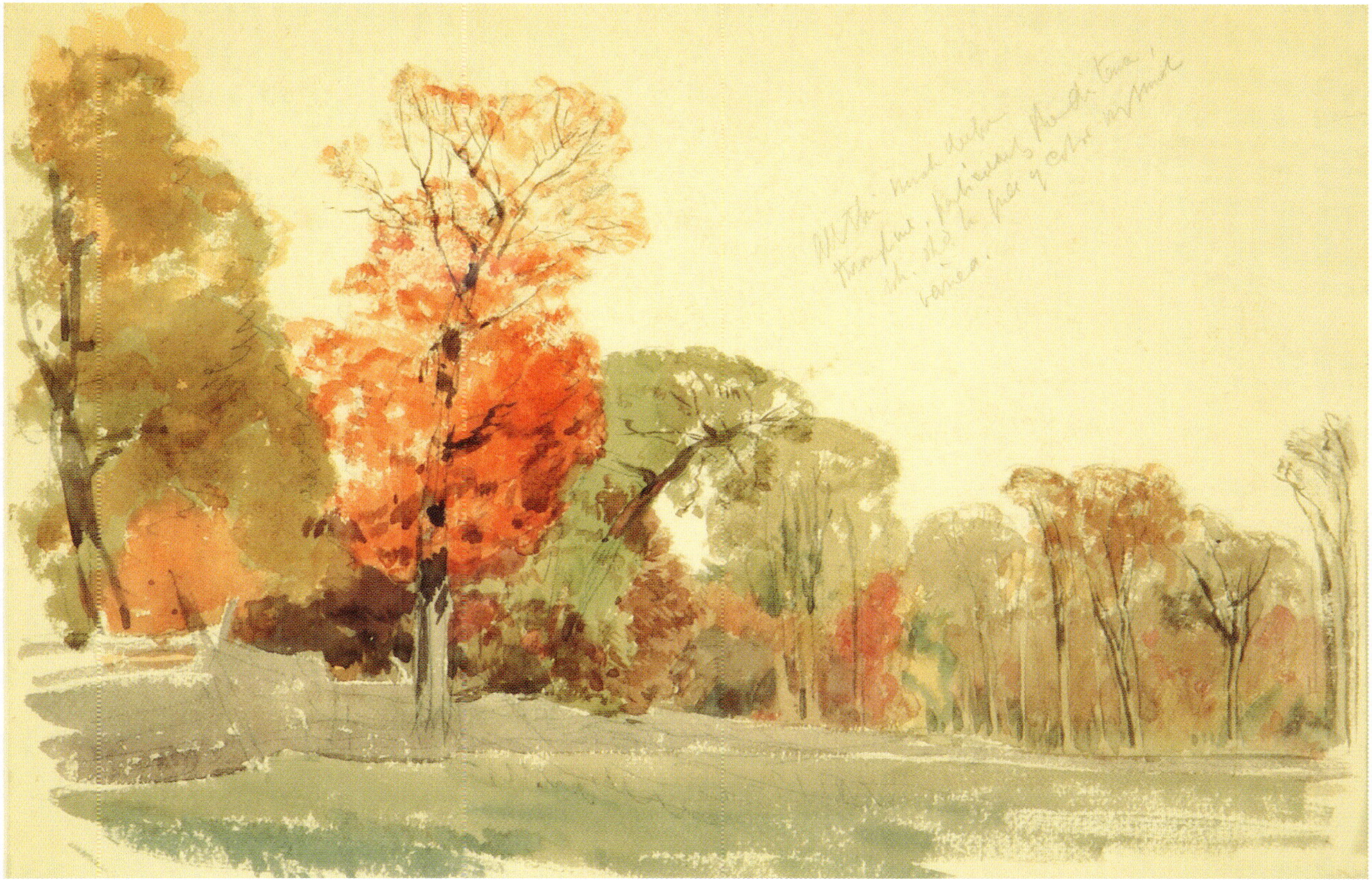

Cat. 54
Fall Woods, Amherst Island, AEAC

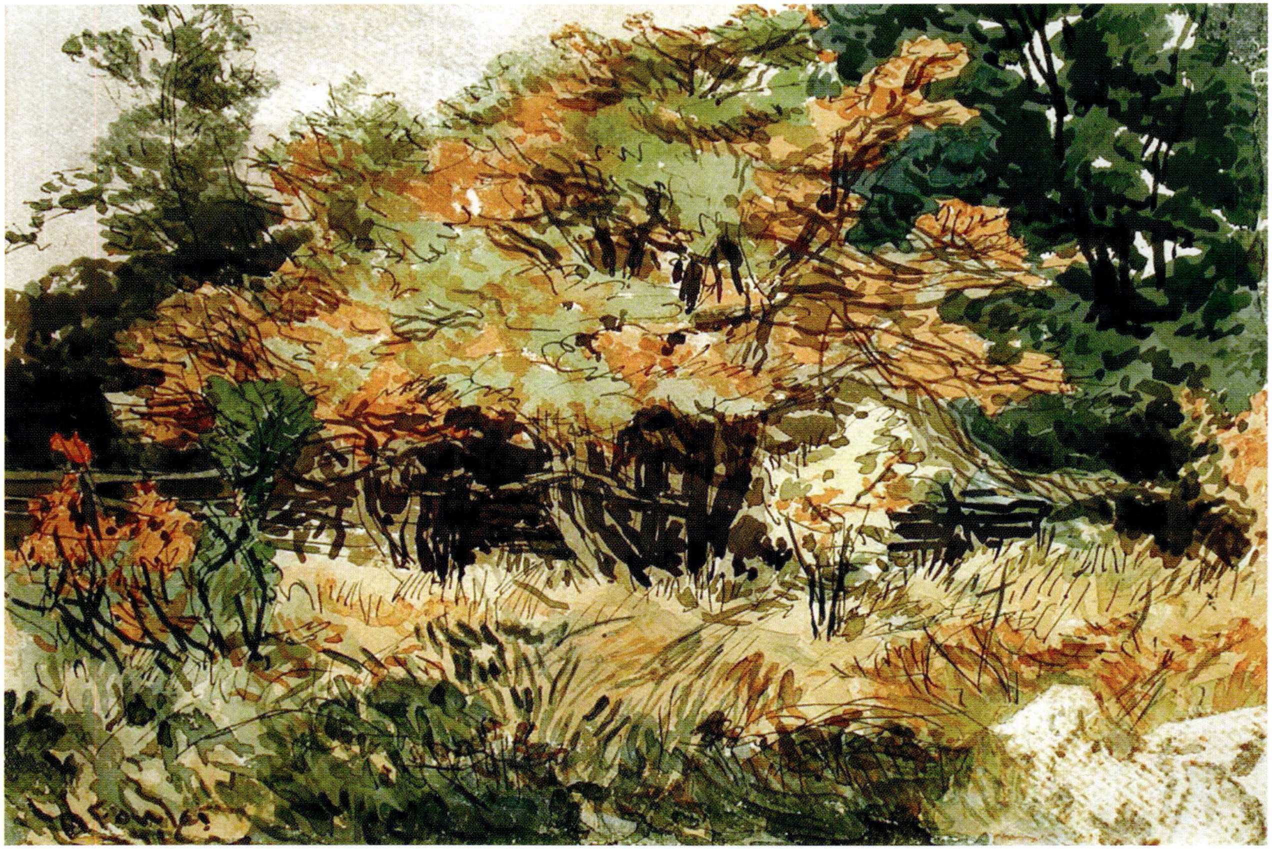

Cat. 24
Early Autumn, 1876, AEAC

the paper wrinkle and the colour run to muddiness. Watercolour medium dries much lighter than applied, and the end result is difficult to predict. Daniel worked the background with dense colour and then, when it was dry, scraped away the surface of the paper to create texture and white highlights. To tear and scrape the paper surface is to court disaster, but Daniel was a master of the technique. This was the famous background technique of which he was so proud.

Dead Canadian Game was included in the first exhibition of the Royal Canadian Academy in 1880. A reviewer remarked:

> Mr. Fowler has here sixteen of his unapproachable [sic, "irreproachable"?] studies of form, colour, and light and shade. I would class them all in the same manner, for whether this talented artist paints a man, a landscape, a flower, or a piece of still life, he treats all with the same intention, merely using them as vehicles to express his extraordinary knowledge and power over his materials, with grand breadth of light and shade and exquisite colour."[10]

The reviewer reveals the kernel of a modern approach to painting. Technical mastery of the depiction of light, shade, and colour is key to the work of many of the great modern painters from Turner onward. One aspect that pleases us today in Daniel's paintings is his modern vision of what makes a painting. What seems dated is the subject-matter of wildlife killed in the hunt, a genre that has passed out of fashion.

Among Daniel's flower pictures a splendid example is *Lilacs (Flower Study)*(cat. 10), a work that may have been in the first exhibition of the Ontario Society of Artists, held in Toronto in April 1873.[11] Again we find the subject placed in the immediate foreground, so we can practically put our noses into the cluster of lilacs. The background is dense, richly coloured, and closed, so the lilacs stand out radiantly in their jar. Daniel wrote: "In flower-painting especially it [the background] is of the last importance: the brilliancy of the transparent colour so exquisite in nature can be got at in no other way."[12] In the flower pieces we discover a debt to the Pre-Raphaelites who had so impressed Daniel in 1860. A central image in opulent colour depicted against a closed background was typical of Pre-Raphaelite composition. Daniel had absorbed the strengths of the Pre-Raphaelites without adopting their dogma, and his work gained greatly by that. He had left his teacher, the tepid Mr. Harding, far behind.

Daniel's struggle to produce a successful landscape came more slowly. He began to sketch outdoors almost daily in good weather. We are fortunate to have an early, unfinished, Canadian landscape study, *Fall Woods, Amherst Island* (cat. 54), which in its incomplete state reveals Daniel's initial struggles to master landscape in colour. A pencil under-sketch blocks in a composition of trees and snake fence seen from a foreground farm field. It is a composition that Daniel would explore throughout his career. The foreground is vaguely washed in, but trees in the background are worked up in some detail. The fence is not picked out and the sky is blank. The study bears a notation: "All this much deeper throughout, particularly the detail wh. wd. be full of colour but much varied." This tentative study has yet to reveal the distinctive broad handling and rich colour that would mark Daniel's mature style.

A later sketch of a similar subject, *Early Autumn* from 1876 (cat. 24), reveals tremendous conceptual and technical strides. It radiates the recognizable style of Daniel Fowler. The compositional focus has moved closer, into the middle and foreground. We no longer stand back to view nature – we are within it with the painter, in a shimmering farm field hard against a dappled wood. The under-drawing is in ink, not pencil. It was a trick Daniel learned from his old friend Edward Lear[13]; it permitted freedom in the manipulation of colour washes without the sketch being lost beneath the watercolour.[14] The paper has the heavy, textured surface that Daniel came to prefer and use to advantage. A rock in the lower right was washed with colour, and the paper, when dry, was scraped, leaving colour only on the crests of the paper's weave. The revealed white of the paper is a perfect means to convey the glare of the midday sun. The composition shows a grasp of the large concept over small detail and brims with confidence. The subject has become heat and light. This is outdoor sketching at its best, although not all Daniel's Victorian critics could appreciate such artistic freedom. A reviewer of the Ontario Society of Artists exhibition of 1877 opined:

> It is rather a pity he is not a little more careful about his work… it is a dangerously facile style to adopt, and in many sketches, Mr. Fowler has been betrayed into a crude, hasty and almost nonsensical scrimmage of colours….[15]

An Inlet, from 1887 (cat. 51), provides a late example. Again the focus is resolutely in the middleground and foreground of the painting. The site is beside the road that passes in front of The Cedars, but the real subject of the painting is the deep, cool shadow that hangs between trees and water. Such transient effects can only be captured by painting rapidly outdoors and are modern in concept. The Impressionists, in their very different way, were chasing light and shadow along the riverbanks of France during this same period. Daniel never ventured the colour theories of the Impressionists, if indeed he ever knew what they were.[16] His method of creating a structure in ink and overlaying it with washes and detail, is a traditional one; his colours, although increasingly rich and interesting, are mixed on the palette and never created by the Impressionists' juxtapositions of brushstrokes of pure colour. Daniel's "impression" of a scene is created by diffusing the viewer's vision through the elimination of detail. The density of shadow is suggested by abstract shapes and rich colour rather than by delineation. The rough paper assists the conceptualization.

These small watercolours differ somewhat from the larger, more highly-worked pieces that Daniel prepared as major exhibition pieces. These were exactly twice the size of his sketches and were worked up indoors under "studio" conditions, sometimes over long periods of time.[17]

Fallen Tree (cat. 34), which was exhibited under the more sentimental Victorian titles of *The Fall and the Fallen*[18] and *How is the Mighty Fallen,*[19] serves as an example. It is painted like a still life. The foreground subject is the exposed root-ball of a fallen tree, very broadly expressed with little detail. It sits in a kind of spotlight against a contrived, almost opaque background of dark but rich colours, the kind of studio concoction that was admired in Daniel's still-life paintings. The blues, reds, greens, and rusts are "Rossetti" colours, the legacy of

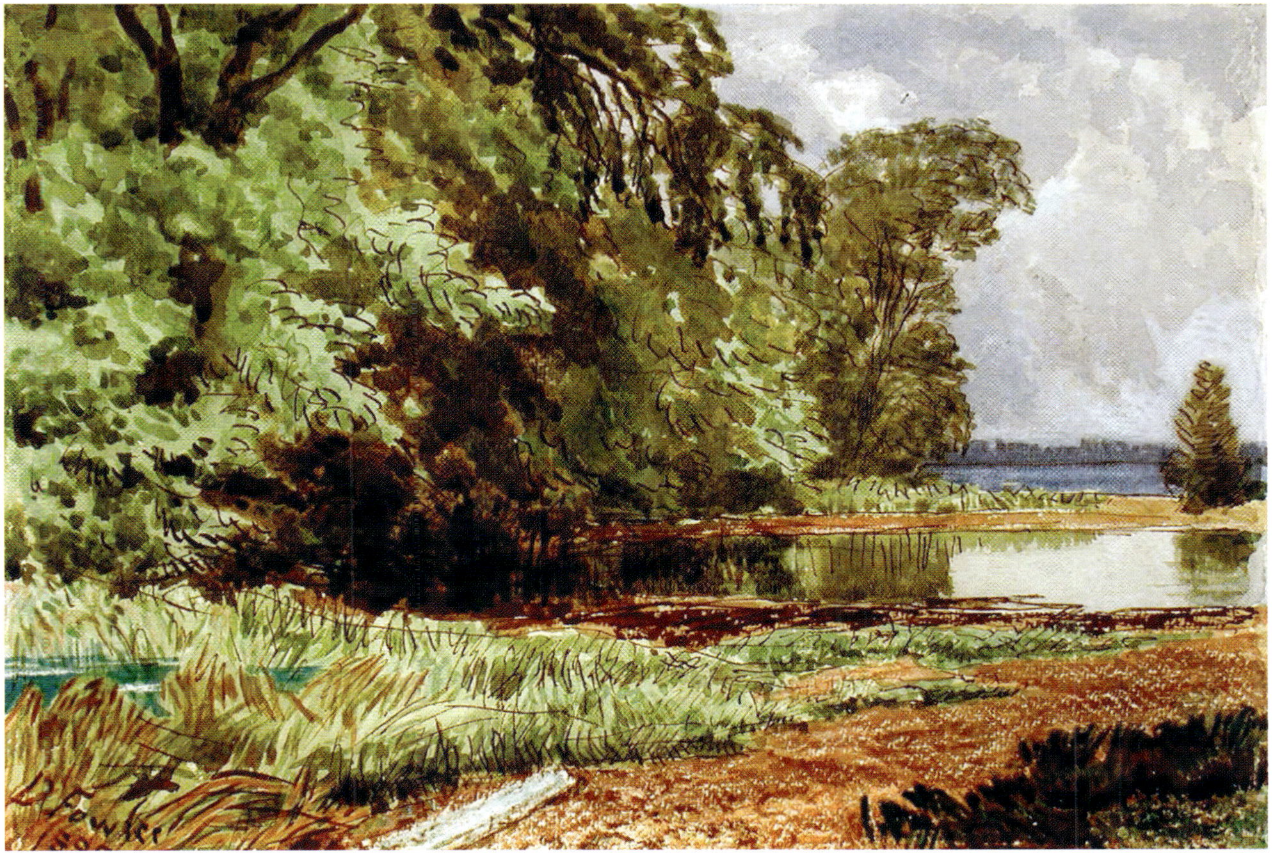

Cat. 51
An Inlet, 1887, AEAC

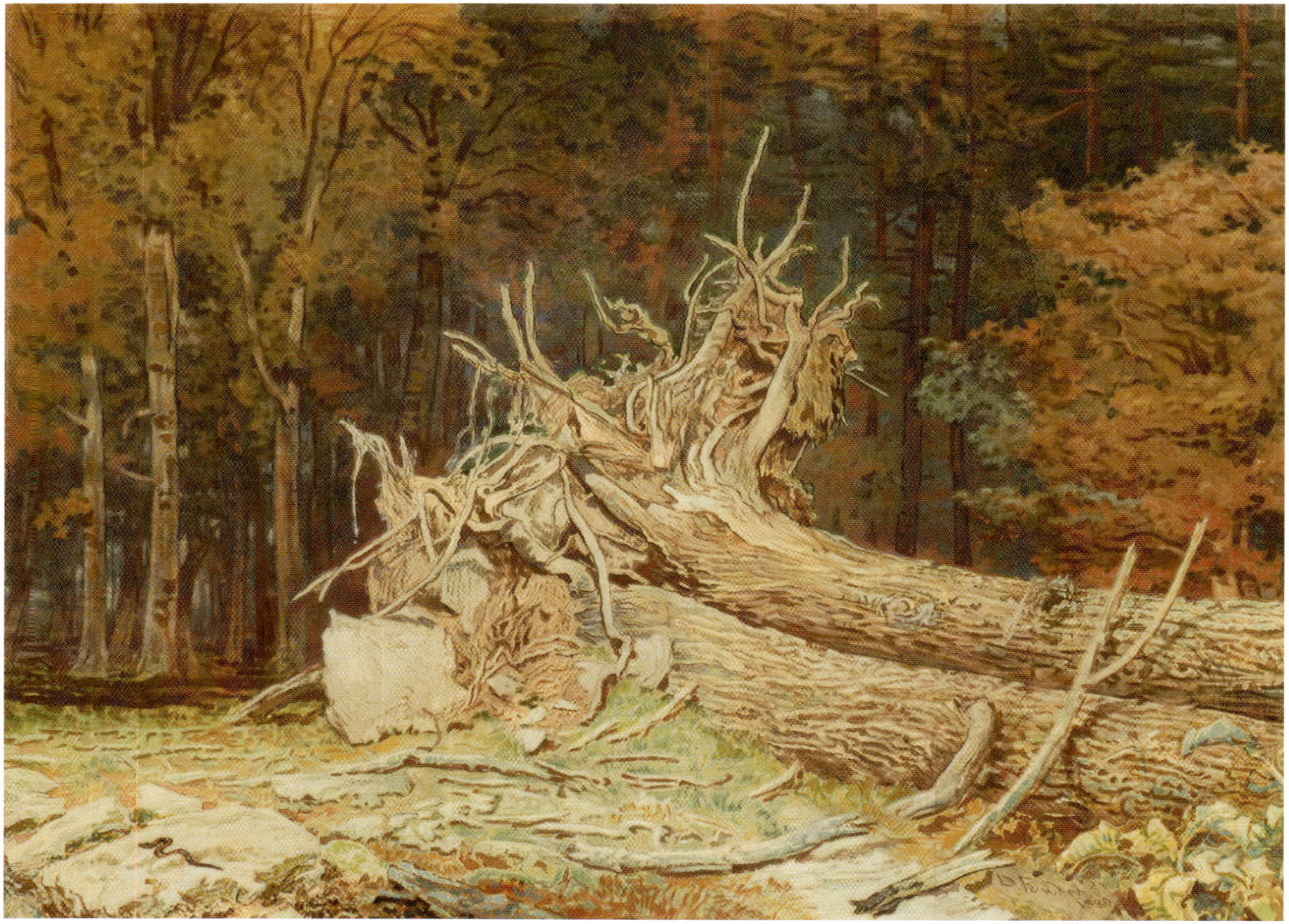

Cat. 34
Fallen Tree, 1880, AEAC

Daniel's interest in Pre-Raphaelitism, as is the bright green where sunlight strikes grass in the foreground. Highlights in the foreground are created by extensive scraping of the paper's surface to reveal white paper beneath. Touches of ink and white paint, applied both under and over the pigment, provide definition.

Today, we tend to prefer sketches to calculated, highly finished works. The more directly and quickly an image is laid down, without second thoughts or self-conscious refinements, the more it speaks to us. This is as true of the sketches of the Group of Seven as it is of works by dyed-in-the-wool Victorians like Daniel Fowler.

What distinguishes Daniel's work from that of his peers and singles him out for special appreciation? A comparison with one of his contemporaries may provide the answer. For example, *The Hunters*, by Allan Edson (1846–1888), in the collection of the Agnes Etherington Art Centre, dates from 1870, when Daniel was beginning to achieve professional recognition. Edson uses smooth paper without the rich texture of the papers that Daniel preferred. The smooth paper permits greater detail, and the structure of Edson's composition is shaped by dainty brushstrokes, not broad masses. Where Daniel saw blues and reds in rotting birch logs and lime greens in young grass, Edson's colour range is restricted to predictable preconceptions of forest colour – soft yellows, greens, and browns. Daniel both perceives more in his subject and is technically abler to present a composition in a vigorous, authoritative manner. Strong colour and broadly massed shapes on the paper's surface give the impression of light, heat, air, and mood. In part this comes from Daniel's deep familiarity with, and affection for, Amherst Island.

In hindsight, it is interesting to examine what Daniel's paintings are not. Although Daniel was an admirer of J.M.W Turner (1775–1851),[20] the raging storms and craggy vistas of the Romantics were not what he wished to depict. Daniel had more wilderness than he wished to contemplate sitting at the edges of his fields. Instead, he memorialized the bucolic, enduring aspects of farm life, the quiet rhythms of rural Canada, picturesque corners with farm equipment buried in long grasses, youngsters bringing the cows home for milking, and the beauties of the water's edge in summer heat. He was not tempted to transform the aboriginal people of his neighbourhood[21] into "noble savages" nor the Québécois raftsmen who sailed past his house[22] into the "jolly habitants" made famous by Cornelius Kreighoff. Daniel articulated the gentle, visual pleasures of his own farm and island.

Most noticeable to Canadians of today, saturated by the ethos of the Group of Seven, is an almost total absence of winter scenes in Daniel's work. This is surprising for a man as obsessed with weather as he was. Like many of us, Daniel enjoyed a measure of his discomfort. His *Journal* of 1862–1863 is full of a farmer's observations on the weather. It reveals him aesthetically responsive to hoarfrost, northern lights, and the other phenomena of our winters. Winter is a relatively quiet time in the life of a farmer, yet Daniel virtually never ventured out into the snow or even to the window to record the beauties of that season. When he speaks of a "sketching season" he means a warm season of the year.[23] In fact, relatively few nineteenth-century landscapists painted the Canadian winter before the 1890s, when Maurice Cullen began to explore the subject. Outdoor artwork could freeze both paint and painter; while winter painting indoors was hindered by poor illumination from oil or gas lamps and fire-light. In any event, the desire to paint the Canadian winter seems not to have existed in Daniel.

Daniel's Colleagues

Daniel Fowler developed his painting style in relative isolation, and for a long time he was largely ignorant of art activities in the primary centres of Toronto and Montreal. Once he began to exhibit, Daniel was quickly taken up by patrons and dealers. Through a favourable review in Toronto, he met George Gilbert, an Australian teacher of drawing and painting at Bishop Strachan School in Toronto.[24] Gilbert eventually amassed a large collection of Daniel's watercolours and helped him market his work. Success came rapidly, and Daniel began to make a little money from his artwork. Eventually, his paintings could also be purchased in Toronto at James Spooner's tobacconist shop-cum-dog-kennel-cum-art-gallery[25]: "Whenever [Fowler] sent a roll of water-colours for framing and sale, Spooner, and Gilbert quarreled over them like dogs over a bone."[26] Daniel was on friendly terms with artist William Cresswell, as noted before, and purchased a painting from him. By picking a quarrel over prize-monies, Daniel became friends with Otto Jacobi (1812–1901), a German artist who settled in Montreal in 1860.[27] Thomas Mower Martin (1838–1934) was another artist Daniel came to know early in his Canadian career.[28] And he certainly would have known, if only by correspondence, the organizers of the annual exhibitions to which he submitted paintings (though his dealer in Toronto, Spooner, sometimes did the submissions[29]). Daniel might read a review but not attend the exhibition. He was not a cultural politician, and he left artistic nation-building to youngsters like Lucius O'Brien (1832–1900) and John Fraser (1838–1898), who were active in the formation of the Ontario Society of Artists and the Royal Canadian Academy. Daniel's rural seclusion and absence from the usual social encounters of the art world bred a mild mystery and awe. So did his age. He was fifty-three years old when he began to exhibit his work in Canada. Most of his fellow exhibitors were a generation younger. At an age when many artists' creative powers begin to atrophy, Daniel's blossomed. Some of his best work was produced in old age, when he seemed to be gloriously free of preconceptions and restraints.

Locally, there were a few artists whom Daniel would have known. Charles Wrenshall (1838–1928) taught art and music in Kingston. Like Daniel, Wrenshall and his three daughters all exhibited in 1893 at the Chicago World's Columbian Exposition.[30] Although documentary proof is lacking, William Sawyer (1820–1889) must have been another local acquaintance. He lived in Kingston from 1852 and was well regarded for his portraits. Forshaw Day (1837–1903) began teaching drawing and painting at the Royal Military College in 1879. Like Daniel, he was a charter member of the Royal Canadian Academy in 1880. Surely they too were acquainted.

To celebrate the founding of the Royal Canadian Academy in 1880, an exhibition of ten diploma pictures was circulated, including Daniel's. One of the venues was Kingston's Mechanics' Institute, which augmented the exhibition with works by Forshaw Day's students, by William Sawyer, and by works belonging to local collectors. The *British Whig* referred to Daniel as "the Father of Canadian

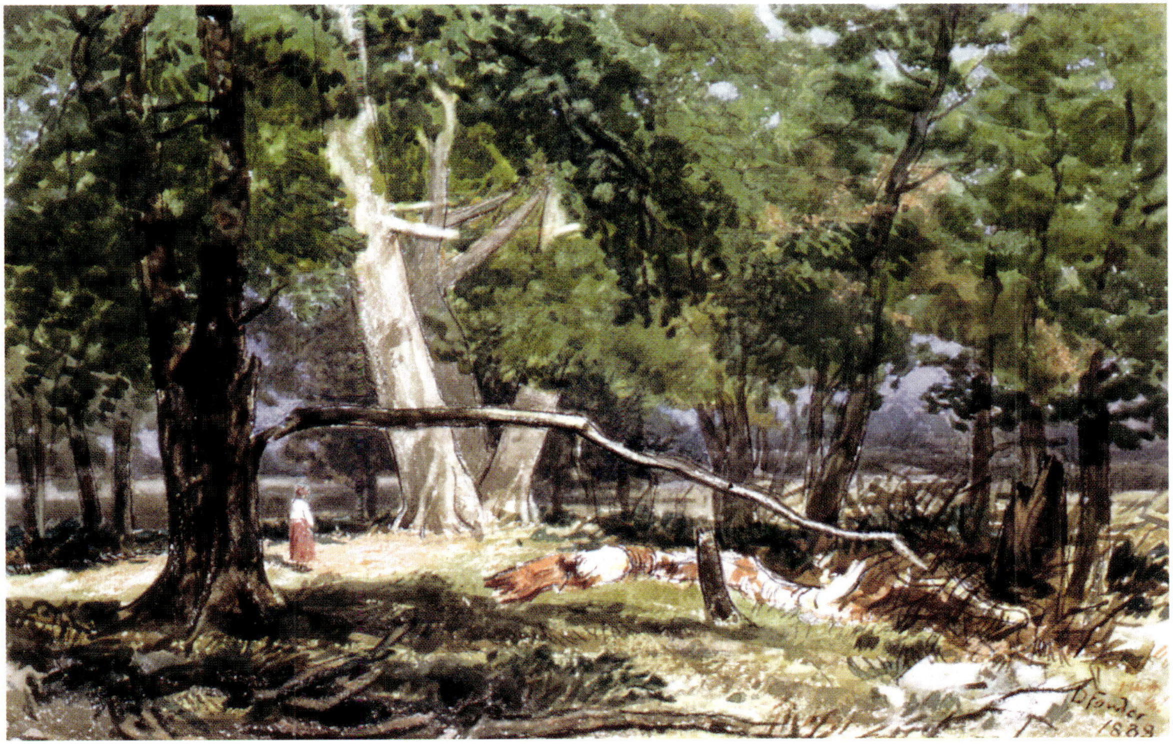

Cat. 52
A Wanderer in the Woodlands, 1888, National Gallery of Canada, Ottawa

art"[31] and mentioned two Fowler paintings that belonged to a local collector, Kingston lawyer R. T. Walkem. Another local patron was Sir Richard Cartwright, Daniel's member of parliament, who owned two Fowler watercolours.[32] It is a pity so little survives to confirm acquaintanceships, possibly even friendships, that must have existed.

1. "The Backwoodsman In England, Part III, by a brother Rustic," manuscript 35-018.08, Agnes Etherington Art Centre (AEAC). The painting is now in the Metropolitan Museum, New York.
2. *Autobiography*, 158.
3. "The Back Woodsman in England, Part III, by a brother Rustic," manuscript 35-018.08, AEAC. The painting was on display at the Goupil Gallery, 168 New Bond St., London in the spring of 1860, when a reviewer described it thus: "Intensity and luminous strength of colour so characterise this picture that at the very first glance we are struck with these qualities, that alone give novelty and power enough to distinguish it from the generality of works of Art…" (*Athenaeum*, 21 April 1860, 549–550). The painting is now in the collection of the City Museum and Art Gallery, Birmingham.
4. *Autobiography*, 157. The Pre-Raphaelite writer William Michael Rossetti, brother of the painter Dante Gabriel Rossetti, phrased it in a very similar way: "'Thoughts towards nature' indicated accurately enough the predominant conception of the Pre-Raphaelite Brotherhood, that the artist, whether painter or writer ought to be bent upon defining and expressing his own thoughts, and that these ought to be based upon a direct study of Nature, and harmonized with her manifestations" (*The Germ, Being a Facsimile Reprint* [London: Stock, 1901], 9–10; cited in David Latham, *Scarlet Hunters: The Pre-Raphaelites in Canada* [Toronto: Archives of Canadian Art and Design, 1998], 7).
5. It was a dark and stormy night on 22 May 1882 when almost no one ventured out to Kingston's Opera House to hear that aesthete descendant of the Pre-Raphaelites, Oscar Wilde, deliver a lecture on "The Decorative Arts." Fowler's article "Your House and Mine: Aesthetic or Not Aesthetic?" appeared in *The Canadian Monthly* the following month. It is tempting to believe that Daniel attended the lecture. However, his article addressed the content of Wilde's other routine lecture, "The House Beautiful," delivered in Montreal on 20 May and in Toronto on 27 May. It would seem that Daniel was writing in response to extensive newspaper reporting of the lectures and to newspaper interviews with Wilde in which Wilde expressed his opinions concerning interior paint colours. For the adventures of Oscar in Kingston and the texts of his lectures, see Kevin O'Brien, *Oscar Wilde in Canada: An Apostle for the Arts* (Toronto: Personal Library, 1982).
6. *Autobiography*, 158.
7. *Transactions of the Board of Agriculture of Upper Canada*, Twentieth Provincial Exhibition, London (Ontario), 1865, Fine Art, 174–176, 176n.
8. At the joint RCA/OSA exhibition of 1885, Daniel exhibited five paintings of European landscapes that he had worked up from old sketches drawn in Europe in the 1830s. One viewer accused him of copying from printed sources. This Daniel stoutly denied, and he was supported by other artists. See Homer Watson to James Spooner, 29 December 1885, and Fowler to James Spooner, 8 January 1886, Colgate Papers, Archives of Ontario.
9. Fowler to James Spooner, 12 October 1885, Colgate Papers, Archives of Ontario.
10. "Academy of Arts. First Public Day of the Exhibition," *Globe and Mail* (Toronto), 9 March 1880, 3.
11. Catalogue number 82, *Lilacs*, priced at $80 and mentioned as *Jug of Lilacs* in the review "The Fine Arts in Ontario," *Canadian Monthly*, III (January–June 1873), 545–546.
12. *Autobiography*, 158.
13. Best known for his *Book of Nonsense*, Edward Lear (1812–1888) met Daniel in the early 1830s in London, where they became friends. Lear made his living as an artist, illustrator, and travel writer. The two remained in touch by letter for the rest of Lear's life. Daniel's copy of Lear's *Rome and its Environs*, a portfolio of lithographs issued in 1841, is now in the collection of the AEAC.
14. *Autobiography*, 161.
15. "Fine Art: The Exhibition of the Ontario Society of Artists," *Canadian Monthly*, XI (January–June 1877), 681–682.
16. "You see no dexterity in nature; you receive impressions. You see nature as a whole and not in parts. If your work comes right as a whole, it must be right in parts. The impressionist order of painters have carried this to a point that the general public eye cannot bear, but their principle is true" (*Autobiography*, 158).
17. In 1870 a reviewer noted: "These two pictures we have seen before but they are much improved; evidently much more thought and time has been spent on them. The artist has disentangled the grouping and produced a pearly quality in the background that is very lovely" ("Review of Fine Arts," *Daily Globe* [Toronto], 5 October 1870).

18. Royal Canadian Academy Exhibition, 1881, no. 88.

19. Owens Art Gallery, St. John, New Brunswick, 1884, no. 35.

20. Daniel described Turner as "the greatest landscape painter that any age or country has produced" (*Autobiography*, 155).

21. Amherst Island is situated near the Iroquois First Nation at Tyendenaga.

22. "This morning a raft passed.... On one occasion we saw one of the French raftsmen walk along a tow rope from the steamer to the raft, half of the line being under water and the whole in motion. Could Blondin have done more?" (*Journal*, 30 April 1863, manuscript 35-018.18, AEAC)

23. *Autobiography*, 107.

24. The dashing Mr. Gilbert also held art classes at his house for "fashionable young ladies and young men of artistic aspirations who wished to make copies of his Fowlers, Millards and Cresswells." Gilbert's wife was a teacher of singing and harp, whose concerts were popular. An incompatible couple, "for long periods they lived separately, and only communicated by spiritual mediums" (Robert F. Gagen, *Ontario Art Chronicles*, typescript, Lorne Pierce Collection, Special Collections, Queen's University Libraries, Kingston).

25. Spooner's was a tobacco shop with a small art gallery at the back. A source of good tobacco, fine paintings, and splendid pointers and setters, seasoned with much gossip, Spooner's was a hang-out for artists and "bloods of the town" (Robert F. Gagen, *Ontario Art Chronicles*, typescript, Lorne Pierce Collection, Special Collections, Queen's University Libraries, Kingston).

26. Robert F. Gagen, *Ontario Art Chronicles*, typescript, Lorne Pierce Collection, Special Collections, Queen's University Libraries, Kingston.

27. *Autobiography*, 165. For another version of the matter, see J.W.L. Forster, "Art and Artists of Ontario," in *Canada: An Encyclopedia of the Country*, ed. J. Castell Hopkins (Toronto: Linscott, 1898), IV, 349–350.

28. "He was one of the first artists with whom I became acquainted" (Fowler to Louisa Murray, 24 March 1894, Fowler Archive, AEAC, photocopy).

29. Fowler to James Spooner, 19 January 1880, Colgate Papers, Archives of Ontario.

30. "Mr. Wrenshall, master of the Art School at Kingston, heard the opinion in Toronto that I had 'not the least fallen off my work'" (Fowler to Louise Murray, 21 April 1890, Fowler Archive, AEAC, photocopy).

31. *British Whig* (Kingston), 14 June 1880.

32. These paintings – *Flowers*, 1874 (cat. 13) and *Woodland Scene*, 1878 (cat.30) – are now in the collection of the AEAC.

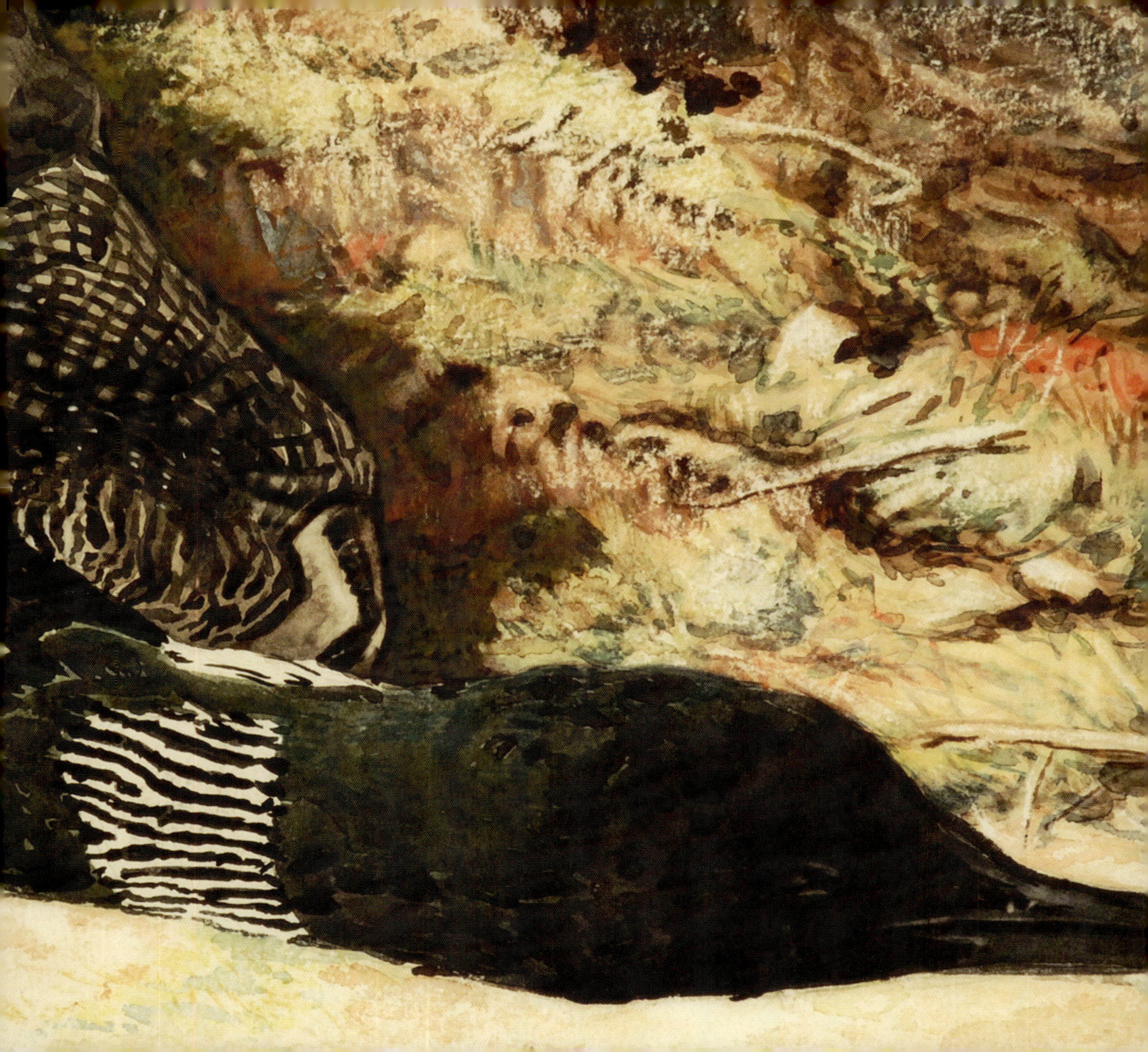

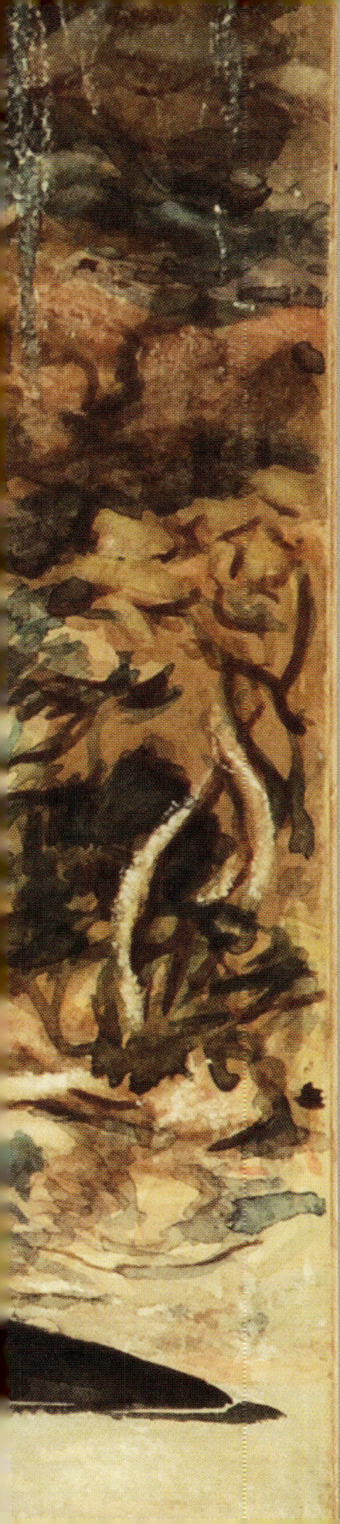

Cat. 40. *Loon*, 1881, Agnes Etherington Art Centre (detail)

The Literary Daniel

I made time, now and then, for writing on any subject, on which I was specially moved to write.

—Fowler, *Autobiography*, 162

The Literary Daniel

During the 1860s, Daniel wrote articles and short fiction that he hoped to publish. An avid reader of periodical literature,[1] he saw an opportunity to join the ranks of authors receiving payment for their work. He wrote factual accounts of life in Canada, fiction based upon events in his own life, more general fiction with Canadian settings, and, in a few instances, fiction set in Britain in past centuries. There is much of interest for the historian in his descriptions of Canadian life. Some of the surviving manuscripts are fair copies Daniel sent to his brother Reginald in England, to be forwarded to publishers. Two were Christmas presents to Daniel's daughters.[2] Alas, for reasons that are glaringly apparent, few were ever published.[3] Daniel's convoluted, cliché-ridden style, and his righteous tone, make many of them difficult reading today. He seems to have had little appreciation for either the cadence or the meaning of language. Later in his life, Daniel had more success with book reviews and letters to the editors of Canadian periodicals.[4]

Undoubtedly Daniel was inspired to write by the success of those close to him. In 1854 his brother Reginald published a travel memoir that included an account of Amherst Island as he discovered it with Daniel in 1843.[5] A longstanding friendship existed between the Fowlers and Louisa Murray, who first published fiction in the *Literary Garland* in 1851.[6] Daniel's daughter Annie Rothwell became a published writer of fiction and poetry during the 1860s. Through Annie he became acquainted with Agnes Machar, who published under the pseudonym Fidelis.[7] There was also the inspiration of literature itself. Daniel, by his own account, was an avid reader, an enthusiasm he shared with his mother and his wife Bessy. He was active in a local book society.[8]

What did Daniel read? Fortunately, a fragment of his library survives intact.[9] On his shelves we find Henry Adams's *Democracy: An American Novel* keeping company with Edward Bulwer Lytton's *The Parisians*, William Thackeray's *The Luck of Barry Lyndon*, Nathaniel Hawthorne's *The House of the Seven Gables*, and Cervantes's *Don Quixote*. Daniel decried the ethics expressed by Wilkie Collins in *The New Magdalen*[10], but he enjoyed Collins's *The Woman in White* and found space in his library for Laurence Sterne's *Tristram Shandy*. He owned a Steeven edition of *The Plays of William Shakespeare*. Travel literature also featured prominently in Daniel's library, including Harriet Martineau's *Eastern Life, Present and Past* and Sir Richard Burton's *Personal Narrative of a Pilgrimage to El-Madinah and Meccah*. Of local interest was *Ocean to Ocean* by George Munro Grant, principal of Queen's College, Kingston, and the *Life and Letters of the Late Hon. Richard Cartwright*. In sum, Daniel was a well-read Canadian.

Daniel is known to have kept journals twice in his life: in 1843, when he briefly travelled westward in Canada West in search of farm property, and made notes for his personal use[11]; and in 1862–1863, when he documented life on a Canadian farm.[12] This latter journal begins awkwardly in a mannered tone that suggests it was intended for publication in England. Daniel provides pseudonyms for his children, defines characteristically Canadian words and habits, with attempts to be witty as well as informative. Over time, however, his entries become the jottings of a genuine journal, the real names of his children replace the pseudonyms, and the entries became ever shorter as Daniel moved from the relative leisure of winter into busier agricultural seasons. The journal is an interesting record, with comments on many topics: the American Civil

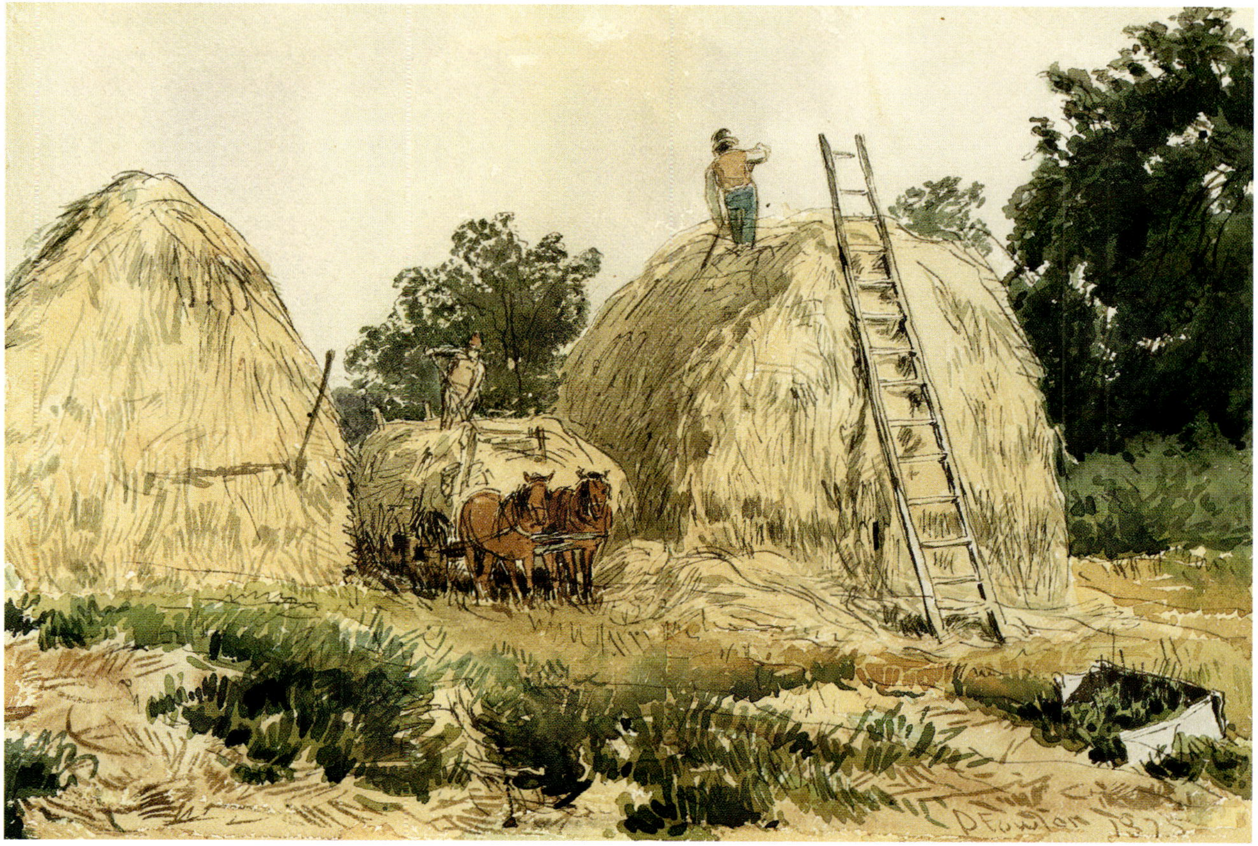

Cat. 14
Haymaking, Amherst Island, 1875, AEAC

War, the death of a neighbour's child (and the scourges of ignorance, poverty, and alcohol-abuse among some of Daniel's neighbours), community balls and dinner parties, spring sowing and planting, summer drought, and the harvest. It is a document of considerable historic interest providing a clear image of Daniel's opinions and personality. Although he wrote this journal during his exploratory period of painting immediately after returning from his second visit to England, he mentions painting only once. On 18 September 1863 Daniel wrote: "Putting the finishing strokes to my drawings for the exhibition, 11 in number."[13] With the submission of these artworks for the Amateur Class of the Provincial Exhibition, held in Kingston that year, painting became the focus of Daniel's attention, and the journal ended with only one further entry.

In the last year of his life, Daniel wrote his *Autobiography*, also intended for publication. Although he left money to finance its publication,[14] his daughter Annie did not have it printed. It was finally published in its entirety only in 1979, as part of the exhibition catalogue by Frances K. Smith for the Agnes Etherington Art Centre. It is a densely written document, somewhat repetitive, and (following the accident that caused Daniel's final decline) was partly dictated. It is the primary source for our knowledge of Daniel Fowler's life, and its charm is that it defined for posterity those things about his life that he wished us to know.

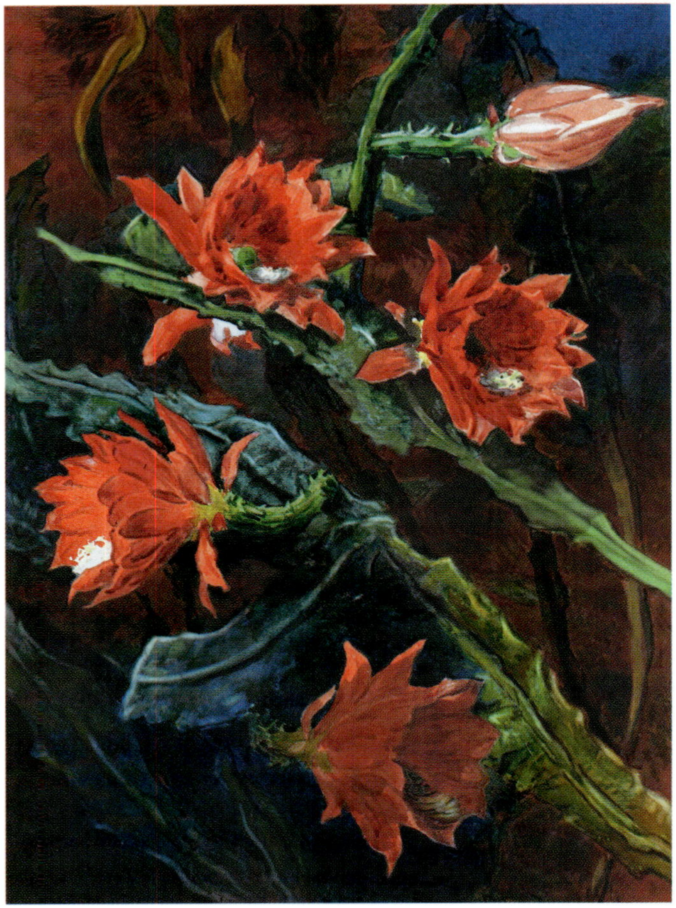

Cat. 22
Cactus , 1875, Art Gallery of Ontario, Toronto

1. The list of British and Canadian periodicals that Daniel read at various times is impressive. It includes *Canadian Monthly, Cornhill Magazine, The Guardian, London Graphic, Magazine of Art, Eclectic, Harper's Magazine, The Mail, The Week, Century Magazine, London Society, The English Illustrated Magazine, Punch's Almanac, Chamber's Edinburgh Journal,* and *The Illustrated London News.* Many would have been periodicals to which Daniel subscribed. Some may have come his way from friends.

2. The short story "Shippegaw, the Indian" has the dedication "Written for and presented to Carry by her father, with best good wishes, Xmas. 1865" (manuscript 35-018.04, Agnes Etherington Art Centre [AEAC]). Carry died from tuberculosis in February 1866. The short story "The Christmas Turkey" is inscribed "Written for and presented to Annie Rothwell by her father with his best love and wishes. Xmas 1866" (manuscript 35-018.54, AEAC).

3. What editor of a periodical would publish a short story titled "The Amputation. In Three Parts" (manuscripts 35-018.38, 35-018.39, 35-018.40, AEAC)? Or enthuse over grammatical errors like "And shave me a 'umstick' cries a shrill curly-headed voice from beside Papa" ("The Christmas Turkey," manuscript 35-018.54, AEAC)?

4. Frances K. Smith cites four articles or reviews in *Canadian Monthly* between 1873 and 1896, and twenty-one articles and letters in *The Week* between 1884 and 1889 (Fowler Archive, AEAC, typescript). For example, Daniel's letter to the editor concerning "Art Criticism" appeared in *Canadian Monthly,* XII (July–December 1877), 103–110; and two of his articles concerning Charles Darwin appeared in *The Week*: "Darwin's Neighbourhood and Neighbours," V,16 (15 March 1888), 197; and "Personality and Character of Darwin," V, 24 (10 May 1888), 381.

5. Reginald Fowler, *Hither and Thither; or, Sketches of Travels on Both Sides of the Atlantic* (London: Frederick R. Daldy, 1854).

6. *Fauna; or, The Red Flower of Leafy Hollow.* Louisa Murray (1818–1894) wrote several other novels serialized in various periodicals. She also contributed to *The Nation, The Week,* and *The Canadian Monthly.* She lived on Wolfe Island for a period of years from 1844, during which time she became a friend of the Fowlers on neighbouring Amherst Island. In the early 1870s Murray moved to Stamford, in western Ontario, but she continued to correspond with the Fowlers until her death.

7. Social activist and feminist writer Agnes Maule Machar (1837–1927) and Daniel locked horns over what Daniel called the "woman question" in a series of letters published in several periodicals. The breach was not mended until Agnes visited him unexpectedly many years later and they spent an afternoon chatting about art. See *Autobiography*, 164, and Fowler to Louisa Murray, 16 January 1891, Fowler Archive, AEAC, photocopy.

8. "Yesterday, that I might not take a horse from the work, I walked to the town wharf, nearly 6 miles, and was thus engaged, on foot, for two or three hours, moving the society book case and books, and re-arranging them. Then I walked the 6 miles home again, carrying a small parcel of books each way. I am home very tired at 7 of the evening" (*Journal*, 24–29 April 1863, manuscript 35-018.18, AEAC). Daniel's experiences in the book society inspired his short story "The Book Society" (manuscripts 35-018.52 and 35-018.53, AEAC).

9. In the holdings of the W. D. Jordan Special Collections and Music Library, Queen's University.

10. Fowler, review of "The New Magdalen. By Wilkie Collins. Toronto: Hunter, Rose & Co. 1873," in "Book Reviews," *Canadian Monthly*, IV (October 1873), 367–359.

11. Thomas R. Lee, "An Artist Inspects Upper Canada: The Diary of Daniel Fowler, 1843," *Ontario History*, L, iv (autumn 1958), 211– 218.

12. *Journal*, manuscript 35-018.18, AEAC.

13. *Journal*, manuscript 35-018.18, AEAC.

14. "And I give to my daughter Annie Rothwell a sum not exceeding three hundred dollars to be devoted to the publishing of my Autobiography" ("Second Codicil to the Last Will and Testament of me, Daniel Fowler of Amherst Island, dated 20 August, 1894," AEAC).

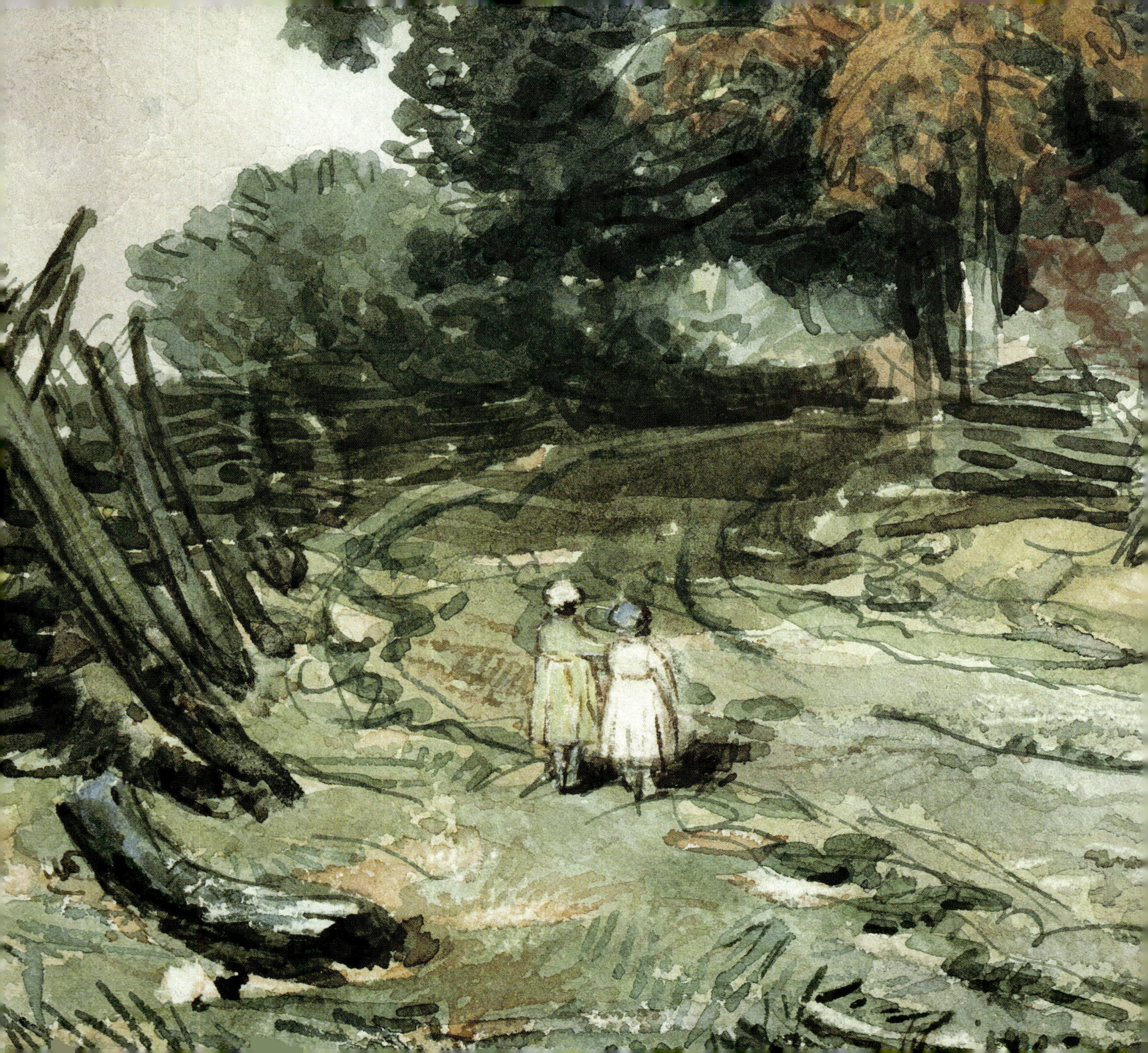

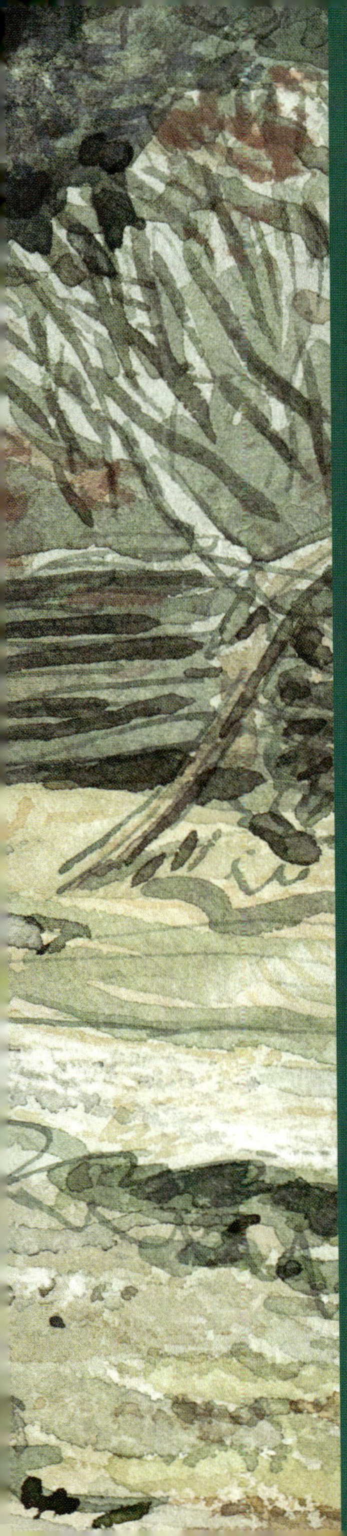

Cat. 26. *Lane with Children, Amherst Island*, 1876, AEAC (detail)

The Cedars

Here, barring the casualties of human life – we have lived in happiness for forty-five years.

—Fowler, *Autobiography*, 147

The Cedars

After running the gauntlett [sic] of five miles of Canadian farm houses, which have little to show in the way of attraction of any kind, it is refreshing after passing through the heart of the beautiful fringe of cedars which skirts the shore for the third part of a mile, to come all at once on a gap where stands a great white gate over which is seen a decidedly ornamental house of this cottage variety. It bespeaks – though I say it myself – the hand of taste and culture.... The pendant frieze or cornice from the eave is particularly effective.

—Fowler, *Autobiography*, 148

From Saturday to Monday I had a blessed little break. Mrs. Rothwell and I took the boat to Amherst Island, where her father lives. We had to drive in the dark of a snowstorm, in a buggy, to the house, under a dark avenue of cedars along the shore, where the waves were foaming and breaking on the broken limestone shore. Then from the cold and snow and dark into a burst of English cordiality and refinement, and Canadian comfort and warmth and ease, and the artistic element that you may imagine would be in the island home of such a first-class but solitude-loving artist as Mr. Fowler.... The original works of art, the books and engravings, the portfolios of sketches, his studio, his books, the grace and beauty of everything, my sweet old-fashioned picture bedroom, and I treated and welcomed as if I had been a long-lost daughter.

—Ada Florence Kinton, *Just One Blue Bonnet*, ed. Sara Randleson (Toronto: William Briggs, 1907), 92 (account from 1885–1886).

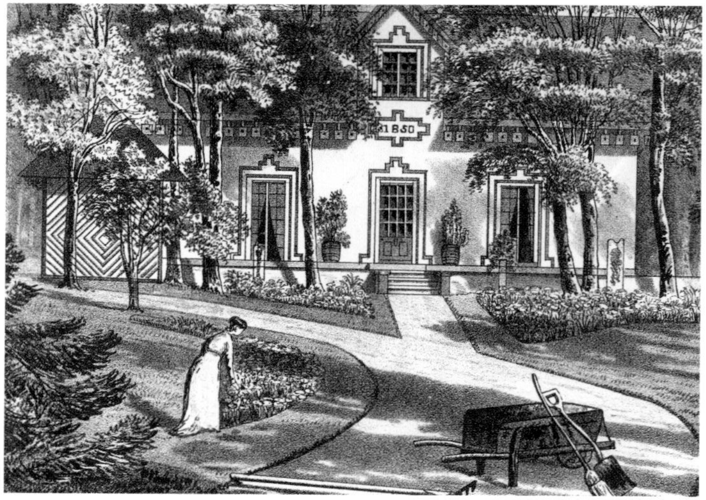

Cat. 31
Residence of Daniel Fowler, Artist, Amherst Island from *Illustrated Atlas of Frontenac, Lennox and Addington Counties, Ontario*, 1878, AEAC

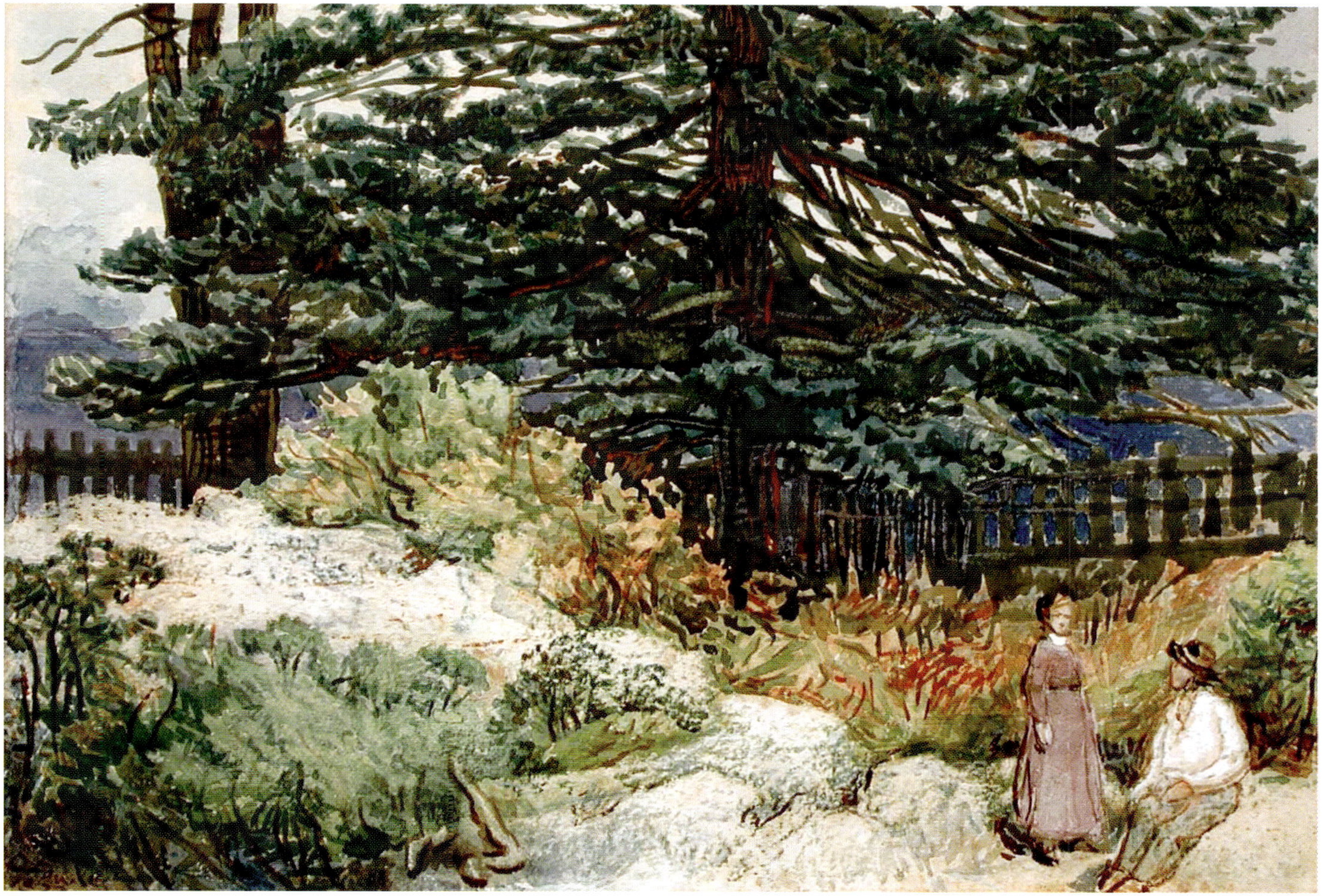

Cat. 29
Evergreen and Rocks, 1877, AEAC

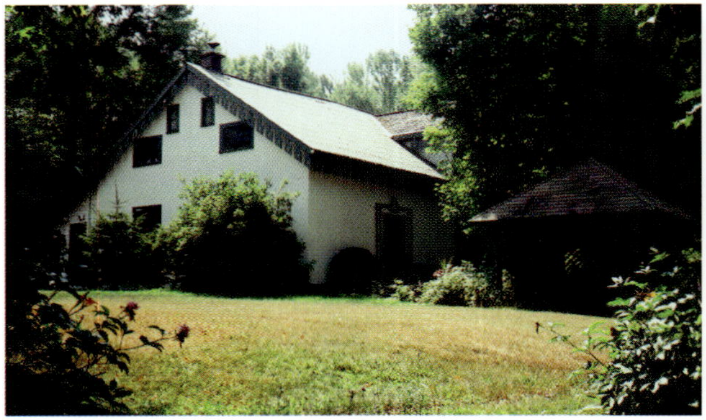

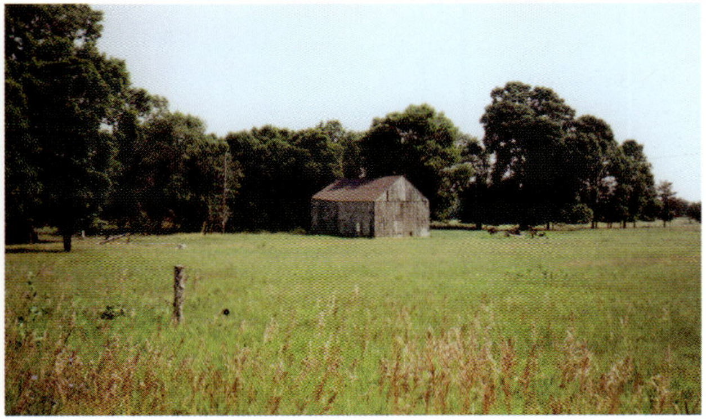

The Exhibition

1. *Allington Castle* (ill. p. 25)
August 1838
watercolour on grey paper
21.6 x 33.7 cm
Agnes Etherington Art Centre, Queen's University, Kingston, gift of Ernest C. Gill, 1966

2. *Design for "The Cedars"*
about 1847–1850
watercolour on cream paper
51.5 x 69.8 cm
Library and Archives Canada, Ottawa

3. *Architectural Drawing*
about 1860
graphite on paper
41.9 x 33.5 cm
Art Gallery of Ontario, Toronto, purchase with assistance from Wintario, 1979

4. *Red Head Duck, Measured Size*
1866
watercolour on wove paper
34.6 x 23.5 cm
National Gallery of Canada, Ottawa, purchase, 1956

5. *Driving Out the Cows*
1867
watercolour on paper
23.5 x 33.6 cm
Collection of Carol Macfarlane

6. *Dawn – Amherst Island*
1867
watercolour on paper
22.7 x 34.5 cm
Collection of Mrs. John Kime

7. *Hollyhocks*
1869
watercolour over graphite on wove paper
71.3 x 50.3 cm
National Gallery of Canada, Ottawa, gift of the Art Association of Montreal, 1918

8. *The Mower*
1871
watercolour on paper
18.9 x 32.7 cm
Art Gallery of Ontario, Toronto, gift from the Fund of the T. Eaton Co. Ltd. for Canadian Works of Art, 1952

9. *The Wheelbarrow*
1871
watercolour on paper
23.2 x 33.2 cm
Art Gallery of Ontario, Toronto, bequest of Dr. John G. Lee, 1955

10. *Lilacs (Flower Study)* (ill. p. 38)
1872
watercolour on paper
48.9 x 34.3 cm
Agnes Etherington Art Centre, Queen's University, Kingston, purchase, Chancellor Richardson Memorial Fund, 1974

11. *Horses and Wagon*
1873
watercolour and brown ink on paper
28 x 38 cm
National Gallery of Canada, Ottawa, purchase, 1988

12. *Fall Scene with Snake Rail Fence*
1873
watercolour on paper
22.5 x 34.2 cm
Collection of Mrs. John Kime

13. *Flowers* (ill. p. 39)
1874
watercolour on paper
33.3 x 23.1 cm
Agnes Etherington Art Centre, Queen's University, Kingston, anonymous gift, 1985

14. *Haymaking, Amherst Island* (ill. p. 55)
1875
watercolour on paper, mounted on card
23.5 x 33.7 cm
Agnes Etherington Art Centre, Queen's University, Kingston, gift of Ernest C. Gill, 1966

15. *Sunset on Amherst Island* (ill. p. 31)
(formerly *Sunrise, Amherst Island*)
1875
watercolour on paper, mounted on card
45.7 x 66 cm
Agnes Etherington Art Centre, Queen's University, Kingston, gift of Ernest C. Gill, 1966

16. *Autumn on the Rideau*
1875
watercolour on paper, mounted on card
18.4 x 33.7 cm
Agnes Etherington Art Centre, Queen's University, Kingston, gift of Ernest C. Gill, 1966

17. *The Broken Tree*
1875
watercolour on paper
24 x 34 cm
Collection of Anna Hitchins

18. *Summer, Amherst Island*
1875
watercolour on paper
23.9 x 33.7 cm
Collection of Anna Hitchins

19. *Woodland with Figure*
1875
watercolour on paper
20.4 x 33.8 cm
Collection of Mrs. John Kime

20. *Bittern*
1875
watercolour on paper
33.7 x 48.2 cm
Agnes Etherington Art Centre, Queen's University, Kingston, gift of Mrs. Allan Walters, 1986

21. *Dead Game*
1875
watercolour on paper
47 x 57.9 cm
Art Gallery of Ontario, Toronto,
gift of Mrs. H. D. Warren and Subscribers, 1919

22. *Cactus* (ill. p. 56)
1875
transparent and opaque watercolour, with gum,
over charcoal on wove paper
48.4 x 34.8 cm
Art Gallery of Ontario, Toronto,
gift of Sir Edmund Osler, 1918

23. *On the Island*
about 1875
watercolour on paper
19.4 x 32.8 cm
Art Gallery of Hamilton,
gift of Mr. and Mrs. Hubert Stitt, 1984

24. *Early Autumn* (ill. p. 42)
1876
watercolour on paper, mounted on card
24.1 x 34.3 cm
Agnes Etherington Art Centre, Queen's University,
Kingston, gift of Ernest C. Gill, 1966

25. *Spring at Adolphustown* (ill. p. 26)
1876
watercolour on paper, mounted on card
23.5 x 33.7 cm
Agnes Etherington Art Centre, Queen's University,
Kingston, gift of Ernest C. Gill, 1966

26. *Lane with Children, Amherst Island* (ill. p. 21)
1876
watercolour on paper, mounted on card
24.1 x 34.3 cm
Agnes Etherington Art Centre, Queen's University,
Kingston, gift of Ernest C. Gill, 1966

27. *Fowler China: Still Life*
1876
watercolour on paper
34 x 48.5 cm
Collection of Roberta Reil

28. *The Oaks*
about 1876
watercolour on paper
28.3 x 39.8 cm
Art Gallery of Hamilton,
gift of Mr. and Mrs. Hubert Stitt, 1982

29. *Evergreen and Rocks* (ill. p. 61)
1877
watercolour on paper, mounted on card
23.5 x 33.7 cm
Agnes Etherington Art Centre, Queen's University,
Kingston, gift of Ernest C. Gill, 1966

30. *Woodland Scene* (ill. p. 8)
1878
watercolour on paper
47.2 x 69 cm
Agnes Etherington Art Centre, Queen's University,
Kingston, anonymous gift, 1985

31 Residence of Daniel Fowler, Artist, Amherst Island (ill. p. 60)
1878
lithograph on paper, as published in *Illustrated Atlas of Frontenac, Lennox and Addington Counties, Ontario* (Toronto: M. H. Meacham & Company, 1878)
28.5 x 37.2 cm
Agnes Etherington Art Centre, Queen's University, Kingston, purchase, 1991

32. *Dead Duck*
1879
watercolour on paper
31.8 x 47.5 cm
Art Gallery of Ontario, Toronto,
bequest of Dr. E. St. George Baldwin, 1931

33. *Dead Canadian Game* (ill. p. 37)
1879
watercolour on wove paper mounted on cardboard
56.2 x 75.3 cm
National Gallery of Canada, Ottawa, Royal Canadian Academy diploma work, deposited by the artist, Amherst Island, Ontario, 1880

34. *Fallen Tree* (also entitled *The Fall and the Fallen* and *How is the Mighty Fallen*) (ill. p. 46)
1880
watercolour on wove paper
45.7 x 61 cm
Agnes Etherington Art Centre, Queen's University, Kingston, gift of Chancellor Agnes M. Benidickson, 1992

35. *Dead Hare in November*
1880
watercolour on paper
48.2 x 70.1 cm
National Gallery of Canada, Ottawa, bequest of the artist, Amherst Island, Ontario, 1895

36. *Wooded Knoll, Amherst Island*
about 1880
watercolour on paper
24.3 x 33.5 cm
Art Gallery of Hamilton, gift of Harold J. Hoffman, 1982

37. *Hickories and Mullins*
about 1880
watercolour on paper
25.6 x 35.7 cm
Art Gallery of Hamilton,
gift of Mr. and Mrs. Hubert Stitt, 1982

38. *Sheep's Hill and Barn, Amherst Island*
about 1880
watercolour on paper
24 x 33.6 cm
Art Gallery of Hamilton,
gift of Mr. and Mrs. Hubert Stitt, 1984

39. *Track Through the Woods, Amherst Island*
about 1880
watercolour on paper
23.4 x 33 cm
Art Gallery of Hamilton,
gift of Mr. and Mrs. Hubert Stitt, 1984

40. *Loon* (ill. cover)
1881
watercolour on paper, mounted on card
33.7 x 47.6 cm
Agnes Etherington Art Centre, Queen's University, Kingston, gift of Ernest C. Gill, 1966

41. *Fallen Birch* (ill. p. 12)
1881
watercolour with white highlights on paper, mounted on card
24 x 34.5 cm
Agnes Etherington Art Centre, Queen's University, Kingston, purchase, Chancellor Richardson Memorial Fund and Wintario, 1976

42. *Slowly Home at Eventide*
1882
watercolour on paper
23.5 x 33.6 cm
Collection of Carol Macfarlane

43. *Green Woods with Figures*
1883
watercolour on paper
23.8 x 34 cm
Collection of Carol Macfarlane

44. *Street at Zell, on the Moselle*
1884
watercolour on paper
68.5 x 48 cm
Agnes Etherington Art Centre, Queen's University, Kingston, gift of Eric Mathews Campbell, M.B.A., 1971, in memory of Group Captain Eric O'Flynn Campbell, M.D., and Genevieve Ardyth (Mathews) Campbell, R.N., 2001

45. *Tree* (ill. p. 10)
1886
watercolour on paper
19.4 x 12.7 cm
Agnes Etherington Art Centre, Queen's University, Kingston, purchase, Chancellor Richardson Memorial Fund, 1973

46. *Fallen Birch*
1886
watercolour on wove paper
49.7 x 70.3 cm
National Gallery of Canada, Ottawa, purchase, 1896

47. *A Rubbish Corner*
1886
watercolour on paper
31.5 x 47.2 cm
Collection of Mrs. John Kime

48 *Woods, Amherst Island*
about 1886
watercolour and ink on paper
35.4 x 25.1 cm
Agnes Etherington Art Centre, Queen's University, Kingston, purchase,Chancellor Richardson Memorial Fund and the assistance of Ken Lawless, 2004

49. *Portrait of the Artist* (ill. p. 14)
about 1886
charcoal on wove paper
35 x 24.9 cm
National Gallery of Canada, Ottawa, bequest of the artist, Amherst Island, Ontario, 1895

50. *An August Noon*
1887
watercolour on paper
31.8 x 47.6 cm
Collection of Susan Kime

51. *An Inlet* (ill. p. 45)
1887
watercolour on paper
24.2 x 34.4 cm
Agnes Etherington Art Centre, Queen's University, Kingston, purchase, Chancellor Richardson Memorial Fund and Wintario, 1977

52. *A Wanderer in the Woodlands* (ill. p. 49)
1888
watercolour over graphite on wove paper
35 x 51 cm
National Gallery of Canada, Ottawa, purchase, 1888

53. *Landscape, Amherst Island (Sandbank with Trees)*
1889
watercolour on paper
23.2 x 32.4 cm
Art Gallery of Windsor, gift of Mrs. J. A. McCuaig, 1980

54. *Fall Woods, Amherst Island* (ill. p. 41)
not dated
watercolour on paper
23.1 x 34.3 cm
Agnes Etherington Art Centre, Queen's University, Kingston, purchase, Chancellor Richardson Memorial Fund and the assistance of Ken Lawless, 2004

55. *Study for Crossing the Ice*
not dated
watercolour on paper
9.4 x 15.5 cm
Agnes Etherington Art Centre, Queen's University, Kingston, purchase, Chancellor Richardson Memorial Fund and the assistance of Ken Lawless, 2004

56. *Sunset, Amherst Island*
not dated
watercolour on paper
12 x 33.2 cm
Art Gallery of Hamilton, William Bullock Bequest, 1980

57. *"The Cedars", Amherst Island*
not dated
watercolour on paper
26 x 35 cm
Art Gallery of Hamilton, gift of Mr. and Mrs. Hubert Stitt, 1980

58. *Wooded Landscape*
not dated
watercolour on paper
19.5 x 33.8 cm
Art Gallery of Hamilton, gift of Mr. and Mrs. Hubert Stitt, 1984

59. *Fishing Boats, Shore, Amherst Island*
not dated
watercolour on paper
24 x 33.7 cm
Collection of Anna Hitchins

60. *Murray's Point, Amherst Island*
not dated
watercolour on paper
20.5 x 30.5 cm
Collection of Anna Hitchins

61. *"The Cedars", Amherst Island*
not dated
watercolour over pencil on paper
33 x 48 cm
Collection of Anna Hitchins

62. *Lychnis and Larkspur*
not dated
watercolour on paper
33.8 x 23.9 cm
Agnes Etherington Art Centre, Queen's University, Kingston, purchase, Chancellor Richardson Memorial Fund and Wintario, 1977

63. Fowler album of sketches
not dated
watercolour on paper
28.5 x 25x 3 cm
Agnes Etherington Art Centre, Queen's University, Kingston, gift of Dr. J. Allen Walters, 1985

64. Fowler's sketching case, with pencil, watercolour paper, and charcoal sketch
17.6 x 12.5 cm
Agnes Etherington Art Centre, Queen's University, Kingston, gift of Jean Johnstone, 1992

65. *Illustrated Atlas of Frontenac, Lennox and Addington Counties, Ontario* (Toronto: M. H. Meacham & Company, 1878)
Special Collections, Queen's University Libraries, Kingston
(See cat. 31)

66. Royal Porcelain Works, Worcester, England
Hand-painted Japanese-style porcelains from the Fowler family set
about 1804
Collection of Anna Hitchins

67. Selection of manuscripts written by Daniel Fowler
1860s
Ink on foolscap
Fowler Archive, Agnes Etherington Art Centre, Queen's University, Kingston, gift of Jean Johnstone 1992

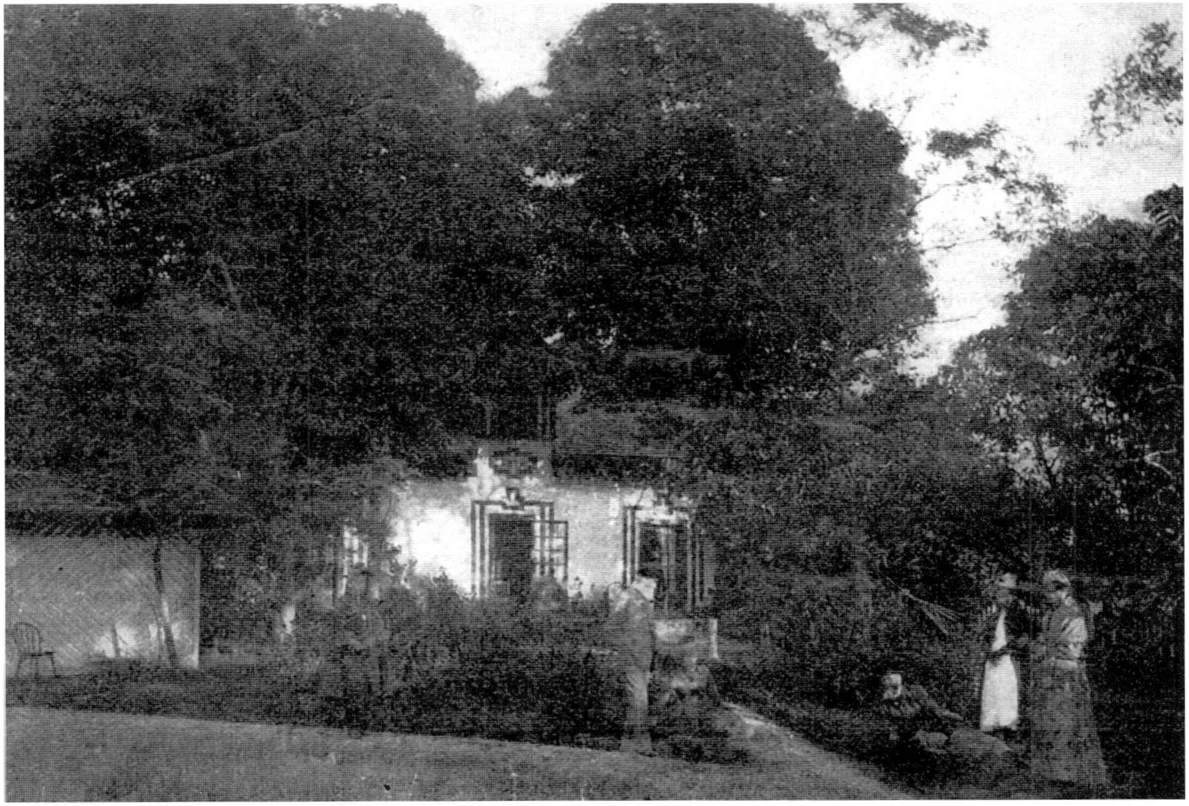

The Cedars, 19th century archival photo from unidentified periodical, Fowler Archive, AEAC

MARQUIS
MEMBER OF SCABRINI GROUP
Québec, Canada
2006